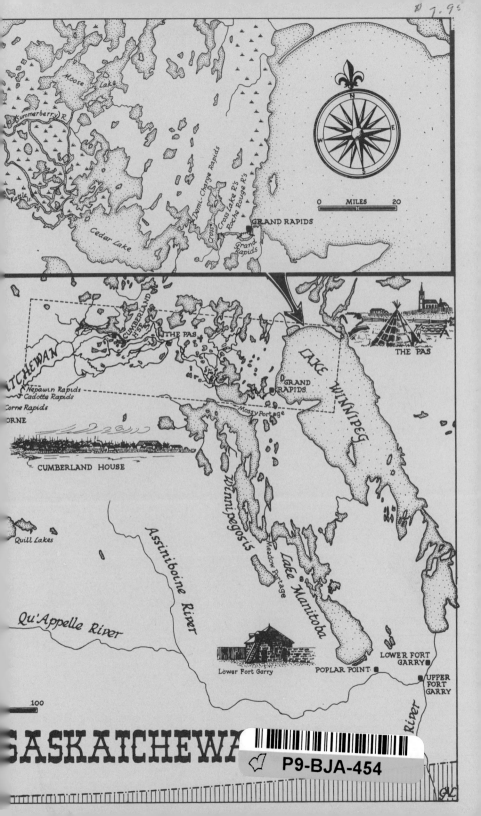

BRUCE PEEL

Bruce Peel was born in southwestern Saskatchewan, so distant from navigable water that in his childhood he was never afloat on anything other than a watering-trough. He has lived since then for many years on the banks of the Saskatchewan, first in Saskatoon, later in Edmonton. The story of the steamboats which plied the 940 miles from Grand Rapids to Edmonton has long fascinated the author, and has led him to search newspaper files and Hudson's Bay Company records for reference to the river boats.

Mr. Peel collaborated with Mr. Eric Knowles, former editor of the Star-Phoenix, in the writing of "The Saskatoon Story, 1882-1953". His major contribution to the history of the West has been "Bibliography of the Prairie Provinces", a source book for scholars, listing early books and pamphlets. In searching for additional titles for inclusion in an enlarged edition the bibliographer in the spring of 1971 visited seventeen European countries in seventy days in search of immigration pamphlets and settlers' memoirs. Mr. Peel edited a collection of essays on his profession under the title "Librarianship in Canada, 1946 to 1967". He has written articles on local and regional history, early western printing, bibliography, and librarianship. He is former president of the Historical Society of Alberta, the Canadian Association of College and University Libraries, the Canadian Library Association, and the Bibliographical Society of Canada.

16/12/71

STEAMBOATS ON THE
SASKATCHEWAN

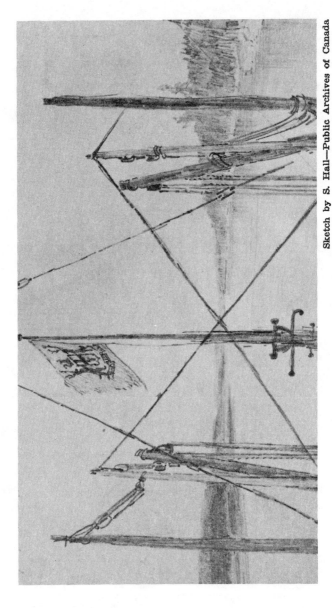

Sketch by S. Hall—Public Archives of Canada

Bow of the NORTHCOTE, the Hudson's Bay Company's flag at her prow, sailing downstream below Carlton House, August, 1881.

STEAMBOATS ON THE SASKATCHEWAN

By Bruce Peel

Prairie Books

THE WESTERN PRODUCER

SASKATOON

1972

DEDICATED
TO MY WIFE
MARGARET

ACKNOWLEDGMENTS

The author gratefully acknowledges the assistance of the following persons who supplied information or clues invaluable in his research. This history could not have been written without the information supplied from the Hudson's Bay Company Archives in London by Miss A. M. Johnson and her staff. The extent to which these archives were used is indicated by the citations in the "Notes." Mrs. Shirlee A. Smith, Librarian at Hudson's Bay House in Winnipeg, provided a copy of all references to steamboats to be found in the Reports of the Governor and Committee to Shareholders, various periodical articles, and several pictures.

Three other archives provided valuable source materials. I am indebted to Mr. Hart Bowsfield, former Provincial Archivist of Manitoba, and his assistant, Mr. Regis Bennett, for providing information on the boats, and on the river captains, most of whom originally were officers on the Red River; Mr. Bowsfield also brought to my attention some short-lived Winnipeg newspapers of the steamboat era in which I found passing references to the Saskatchewan boats. Mr. Alan R. Turner, Provincial Archivist of Saskatchewan, sent me material and pictures. from the archives in Regina. Mr. James Dunn, Chief Librarian of the Minnesota Historical Society, provided me with a microfilm copy of the series of newspaper articles by George B. Merrick on "Steamboats and Steamboatmen of the Upper Mississippi." Mr. Eric Knowles, former Editor of the **Saskatoon Star-Phoenix,** kindly supplied material on the voyage of the **Lily** up the South Saskatchewan, and some pictures.

Finally, I acknowledge the help given to me, in letters and in an interview, by Mrs. Jessica Watson, of Vancouver, the nonogenerian daughter of Captain J. S. Segers. Although her personal acquaintance with steamboating was limited to the Athabasca River, she could recall stories her father had told her of his earlier riverboat experience.

In addition to those people who provided information, I am indebted to a number of people who supplied pictures: Mr. Georges Delisle, Chief of the Picture Division, Public Archives of Canada; Mr. S. Whitaker, Public Relations Department, Manitoba Hydro; Dr. Y. O. Fortier, Director, Geological Survey of Canada; Miss G. M. Chagnon, Education Section, National Museum of Canada; Mr. Ron Vastokas, of Toronto; Mr. Ted Tadda, of Cranberry Portage; and Mr. Richard Harrington, of Toronto. For the excellent cartography I am indebted to Mr. G. A. Lester, cartographer at the University of Alberta.

Bruce Peel,

Edmonton, 1972

TABLE OF CONTENTS

ILLUSTRATIONS

MAPS, TABLES, ETC.
(*Cartography by G. A. Lester*)

INTRODUCTION

The Hudson's Bay Company, from the opening of its first post inland from the Bay—Cumberland House, in 1774—depended on canoes and, later, York boats to transport trade goods into and furs out of the vast hinterland. A century later, in the early 1870's, the Company introduced steam navigation on some of the main transportation routes. At the same time York Factory on Hudson Bay lost to Fort Garry on Red River its pre-eminence as the fur trade entrepôt.

The Company placed its first steam vessel on Lake Winnipeg in 1872 to carry goods between Fort Garry and the mouth of the Saskatchewan River. One of the first cargoes was the lumber and machinery to construct a sternwheel steamer above Grand Rapids which obstructed the mouth of the Saskatchewan. The first riverboat was launched on the river in ·1873 and promptly wrecked, but was replaced the following year by the famous **Northcote**. A second riverboat, the **Lily**, was assembled above Grand Rapids in 1877. Five years later the Winnipeg and Western Transportation Company transferred three boats from the Red River to the Saskatchewan. These were the **Manitoba**, the **North West**, and the **Marquis**.

Trade goods destined for the Far North were disembarked from the Saskatchewan steamers at Carlton House and from thence transported overland to Ile-à-la-Crosse and on by water, over Methy Portage, then down the Clearwater River to Fort McMurray on the Athabasca River. Here, in 1883, a sternwheeler, the **Grahame**, was launched to carry goods down the

Athabasca River, across Lake Athabasca, and down the Slave River as far as the rapids above Fort Smith. At Fort Smith, in 1887, a steamboat, the **Wrigley,** was built to carry goods down the Slave-Mackenzie river systems. More important to the story of the Saskatchewan River steamboats was the building of the **Athabasca,** also in 1887, on the upper part of the river of the same name, at Athabasca Landing north of Edmonton. Edmonton had become the entrepôt for the north country.

This narrative is confined to steamboat navigation on the two branches of the Saskatchewan. The rapids, sand bars, shallow channels, and irregular flow made it a difficult river to navigate. Perhaps on no other river in the world were paddle-wheel steamers sailed so far on such a shallow flow of water. The river was difficult to navigate under the best of conditions; in the early eighties, along an isolated stretch above Cumberland House, the old channel for fifty miles was being abandoned for new channels where the river became lost in a vast reed-swamp west of Cumberland Lake. Success in an upward voyage with a heavily laden boat had always been a gamble; now the odds were stacked against getting through, and the steamboats which had plied the 940 miles from Grand Rapids to Edmonton were beached, or diverted to short runs on stretches of the river.

Some day archeologists searching along the river may find pieces of hulls or machinery. The **Lily** went to the bottom at Drowning Ford below Medicine Hat in 1883. The **Manitoba** was crushed by ice in her winter quarters at the mouth of the Sturgeon River above Prince Albert in the spring of 1885. The **Northcote** was beached at Cumberland House in 1886. The **Marquis** slowly went to pieces on the bank at Prince Albert until finally dismantled to build a family residence. The **North West** ended her career dramatically when she broke her moorings at Edmonton during a summer flood in 1899, and crashed into the piers of a bridge under construction.

In later years other steamboats operated on the Saskatchewan, but not all were paddlewheelers and none was as large as the early boats. Most plied only short stretches of the river. The Pas was home port for most of the latter boats. In the spring of 1954, at The Pas, the **David N. Winton,** last of the steam-driven sternwheelers, was sunk by the action of ice.

The story of steamboats on the Saskatchewan is one of men and boats pitted against the perversity of an unpredictable river.

Chapter 1

THE RIVER

THE SASKATCHEWAN RIVER with its great
length, and two branches, would seem to be
a mighty waterway on a map of the Prairie
Provinces. But, like all rivers flowing through the
plains region of North America, its volume of water
is relatively small. The early river captains found the
depth barely sufficient for their light-draft vessels
except when the melting snows in the mountains in
June, or heavy rainfall in the upper country, raised
the level above the normal flow.

The Saskatchewan, from its mouth on Lake
Winnipeg to the head of navigation at Edmonton
on the north branch, could be divided into five sections, each with its own characteristics. Working up-
river, as would an upbound boat, the sections were as
follows. The river in the last 30 miles of its flow
came tumbling down across a corner of the Pre-
cambrian Shield in a series of rapids culminating in
Grand Rapids, where the river fell nearly 80 feet in
3 miles. The latter being an insurmountable barrier,
the steamboat wharf was located above it. The second
section of the river, about 240 miles in length, flowed

through flat, marshy country. Since the channel was deep, this portion of the river was the best suited for navigation, except near the upper end. Here, at a point called The Cut-Off, the river had broken through its low banks into the Sturgeon River system to the north and was losing its waters in a vast swamp which lay to the west of Cumberland Lake. In the third section of the river six rapids occurred within 170 miles. Of these rapids, the most difficult for steamers to ascend were the Thorburn (or more commonly called Tobin's) Rapids, and above the Forks of the two branches of the river, a series called Cole's (more properly La Colle) Falls, marked on present-day maps as Cole's Rapids. In the fourth section, from Prince Albert to the confluence of the Vermilion

THE RIVER

TABLE OF DISTANCES

MAIN RIVER	
Grand Rapids (foot of)	0
Grand Rapids (head of)	3¾
West end of Tramway (Steamboat dock)	4⅜
Dock for Steamboats	0
Roche Rouge Rapids	3⅞
Cross Lake Rapids	5⅜
Cross Lake	12⅞
Demi-Charge Rapids	13⅜
Cedar Lake (East End)	33⅝
Moose Lake River	67⅝
Kettle Island	76
Moose Lake River	121⅛
The Pas	139⅝
Tearing River	206⅞
Cumberland House	209⅜
Big Stone River	216⅝
Big Niggar Bar	254⅞
The Cut-Off	270⅛
Sepenoch Channel	273⅝
Squaw Rapids	284⅝
Thorburn (Tobin's) Rapids	289⅛
Big Birch Island	300
Pemmican Point	300¾

Rowan's Island	301¾
Devil's Point	314¾
Nepawin Rapids [sic]	333¼
Cadotte Rapids	336½
A La Corne Rapids	379⅞
Fort à la Corne	384⅞
The Forks	409⅜

NORTH BRANCH (Distances approximate only)

The Forks	0
Cole's Falls	9
Prince Albert	39
Carlton House	89
Battleford	202
Fort Pitt	308
Moose Rapids	354
Dog Rump Rapid	367
Eye Rapid	398
Crooked Rapid	425
Victoria Rapid	452
Jump-Off Rapid	478
Stony Bar Rapid	512
Edmonton	530

SOUTH BRANCH

The Forks	0
Medicine Hat	615

River, the North Saskatchewan ran in a wide gravel bed marked by islands and shifting sand bars. For the remaining distance to Edmonton the channel was reasonably straight, with an adequate depth of water.

The accompanying table of distances indicates the principal rapids and other points along the Saskatchewan and its two branches.

The Hudson's Bay Company, petitioning the Dominion Government in 1879 to make improvements in the river, listed the obstacles which were most troublesome to navigation.[1] The petition asked that piers be built at the heads of Roche Rouge and Demi-Charge rapids so that a shorter hawser might be used in warping the steamers up; at the former rapids a

3

pier would reduce the line used from 3,000 feet to 2,000, and at the latter from 6,500 feet to 2,000. At both Thorburn Rapids and Cole's Falls, boulders needed to be removed from the navigable channel, and wing dams constructed to narrow the channel and thus deepen the flow of water.

The Cole's Falls series of rapids constituted the most serious obstruction to navigation. The fourteen short rapids* had a total fall of 87.5 feet in 13 miles; the fall in the rapids proper amounted to 50 feet, the remaining fall was in the intervening "swifts." The river bed here was considerably constricted, varying in width from 400 to 800 feet in low water, and it had a number of sharp bends. Most of the rapids were located in the bends, and here the boulders brought down by ice from higher reaches tended to accumulate. Navigation of this stretch of river was hazardous at all times, but in low water it was impossible to warp steamers up. Many an upbound voyage ended at the foot of Cole's Falls.

The great variation in the flow or water level of the river from week to week, and from season to season, made the outcome of every upbound voyage unpredictable. Would the level hold all the way to the boat's destination? If the water were in low stage, should the steamer struggle on over shoal and sand bars in the expectation that a crest of higher water might be met? If the rise did not occur, the boat had to unload its cargo on the bank and return downstream.

The water in the Saskatchewan usually rose with

*E. A. Burbank later listed twenty rapids, but he probably counted some of the "swifts" between.

the spring break-up of the ice, then fell, and in mid-summer reached its highest level. The flow during the second rise was influenced by the weather in the Rocky Mountains; the river was high when the midsummer sun melted a greater volume of snow, or when warm rains fell in the mountains. For instance, the weather in 1883 was so cool and cloudy that little high-altitude snow melted, and as a result no summer rise in the water level occurred; that year navigation was a failure. The midsummer rise was important to river navigation, for the higher level of water and its duration determined the length and success of the navigation season.

Was the Saskatchewan navigable? Two out of three voyages up-river were tales of tribulation, but if successful, a steamboat could bring to Edmonton as much freight, only a month out of Winnipeg, as a cart train of 150 to 200 carts could move across the plains in a summer. The answer was given by the **Bulletin** of Edmonton in its issue of November 5, 1881:

The Saskatchewan is considered by some not to be fit for navigation but it must be very bad indeed if it is not better than slow going oxen on a muddy road one thousand miles long.

From Robert H. Hill: Manitoba, history of its early settlement, development, etc.

The ox train was the alternative to moving freight by boat from Winnipeg to Edmonton. Each cart carried half a ton so that it took 200 to 400 carts to carry as much freight as one sternwheeler if the water of the Saskatchewan was in good stage. This illustration shows the last ox train to pass through Portage la Prairie.

Chapter 2

EARLY SURVEYS OF THE RIVER

T HE FIRST SCIENTIFIC MAN to ascend the Saskatchewan River and comment on its suitability for steam navigation was a member of the Palliser exploratory expedition sent to Rupert's Land by the British Government in 1857. Lieutenant (later Captain) Thomas Blakiston of the Royal Artillery, the expedition's magnetic observer, entered the country by way of York Factory because it was thought that it would be less hazardous to transport the delicate survey instruments by York boat than by cart from Fort Garry. Blakiston's observations of the navigability of the Saskatchewan were based on his upward journey in October, 1857, as far as Carlton House, and on his downward progress from Edmonton to Carlton House almost a year later. Thus, his experience on the river was at a season when the flow of water was normally low.

Blakiston questioned whether Thorburn Rapids could be climbed by steamer even in high water, but he thought Nipawin Rapids could. Of Cole's Falls, he said that it was impassable in low water, but added "those who have seen these rapids at high water think they would be no obstruction."

Blakiston's report on the navigability of the main and north branch of the Saskatchewan concluded on a skeptical note:

> Of the distance to which a steamer would ascend in high water, I can give no positive information, but I should suppose that one adapted to that kind of navigation might possibly reach Fort Edmonton, but in low water little could be accomplished in most parts.[1]

Donald A. Smith (later Lord Strathcona), speaking in the House of Commons on the first successful navigation of the Saskatchewan by the steamer **Northcote,** was no doubt alluding to the Blakiston report:

> Though I have great respect for scientific men, I am bound to say that if the Hudson's Bay Company had been guided by the reports of engineers, they never would have dared to launch a steamer on the Saskatchewan. Other persons reported that the river was navigable, and took the responsibility of building a steamer at a cost of fifty or sixty thousand dollars.[2]

As a footnote to Thomas Blakiston's exploration in the Canadian West, it is interesting that he sought permission to make a solo canoe voyage down the South Saskatchewan. Permission was refused by the expedition's leader, Captain John Palliser, who considered it too dangerous for one man to canoe down an unknown river. This was one more of the differences of opinion which separated Blakiston from the other members of the expedition, and at the end of the summer of 1858, he resigned and left the country.

He refused to hand over his observations and maps for incorporation in the expedition's report.

Captain Blakiston rejoined his regiment, which had been posted to Hong Kong; here, within a few months, he was off on a one-man exploration of one of China's great rivers, the Yangtsze Kiang. In 1862, he published a book, **Five Months on the Yang-tsze,** which for nearly fifty years remained the main source of information on the topography and natural history of the regions drained by that great river.[3]

The second survey of the lower or main Saskatchewan was made in the summer of 1858 by John Fleming, a member of the H. Y. Hind Assiniboine and Saskatchewan Exploring Expedition sponsored by the Canadian Government. Fleming boated downstream from the Elbow of the South Saskatchewan. His comments on the navigability of the river were confined to the rapids near the mouth of the river. He was of the opinion that powerful steamers could ascend the Roche Rouge, Cross Lake, and Demi-Charge rapids under their own power. His silence on the navigability of the river above suggests that he assumed it navigable once the lower rapids had been climbed.

Grand Rapids was a barrier to steamboats entering from Lake Winnipeg. Fleming commented as follows:

To navigate the Saskatchewan at present, a steamer would evidently have either to be built above the rapid, hauled over the portage, or warped up the rapid itself. Seeing that the Company's large bateaux are hauled up the rapid by

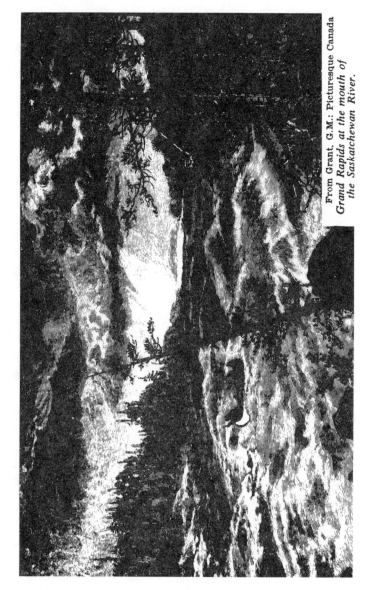

From Grant, G.M.: Picturesque Canada
*Grand Rapids at the mouth of
the Saskatchewan River.*

manual labour, it does not seem impracticable for an empty steamboat, with engines of great power, to ascend it, by the aid of hawsers and guy-ropes stretched from the steamer to the land, using, along with capstans, the motive power of the steamer as far as available.[4]

At Cross Lake, the explorer met the Hudson's Bay Company's Saskatchewan brigade of fourteen boats bringing up the fall outfit of goods. Chief Factor Wm. J. Christie, of Edmonton, in charge of the brigade, hoped that the "long-talked-of steamers" would soon make their appearance on Lake Winnipeg, thus shortening the annual journey of the fur brigades.

The third report on the navigability of the river was made by two steamboat men from the Red River, on a survey instituted by the Hudson's Bay Company. The surveyors were Captain Silas Munn and Pilot E. R. Hutchinson of the steamer **International.** They traveled up-river in a rowboat as far as Carlton House in October, 1865. The river was low and beginning to freeze over, so the travelers completed the journey only with difficulty.

Captain Munn's report described the river as a good navigable stream from Grand Rapids to Thorburn Rapids. From that point to Carlton House he did not find the river navigable in October, but he had been assured by Chief Trader Arthur Pruden, of Carlton House, that the water was three and one-half feet higher from June 1 to September 15. Munn's conclusion was that "with this additional water, I am of the opinion that light draught steamers could be sent as far as I explored it without any serious difficulty." The captain noted that the river was well wooded, affording an abundance of cordwood with which to stoke the steamers' furnaces.

The one improvement Munn recommended in the river was the sinking of a pier at Cross Lake so that a hawser could be attached to help an upbound steamer climb Cross Lake Rapids to enter the lake. He found these rapids to have a narrow steamboat channel, and a thirty-inch drop in a distance of ten chains.[5]

Eight years were to elapse after the Munn-Hutchinson report before the Company made an attempt to place a steamboat on the river.

Of the later surveys of the Saskatchewan River, the first was by E. A. Burbank, Superintendent of Saskatchewan River Improvements, who made a detailed report on the north branch in 1883 and of the lower portion of the south branch in 1884.[6]

In the summer of 1884, Otto Klotz went downstream from the Elbow of the south branch to the mouth of the main river. His survey, narrative, and photographs are a valuable contribution to our knowledge of the river in the steamboat era.[7]

The most exhaustive survey of the Saskatchewan River system, from Rocky Mountain House to Grand Rapids, was made under the direction of L. R. Voligny for the Dominion Department of the Interior over several seasons from 1910 to 1915. Voligny's report suggested that construction of a number of dams would raise the water level sufficiently so that flat-bottomed grain barges could be used to move grain down-river toward the European markets.[8]

Chapter 3

THE COMPANY CHANGES ITS
TRANSPORT ORGANIZATION

T HE PLACING of a steamboat on the Saskatchewan River was part of the reorganization of
transportation routes and methods by the
Hudson's Bay Company. The factors influencing these
changes were three. The first was the recognition of
the strategic importance of Fort Garry as an entrepôt
for goods entering the country; once steamboats were
used to bring goods down the Red River it was logical
to extend their use across Lake Winnipeg and up the
Saskatchewan River. A second factor was the growth
of settlement along the Saskatchewan and the need for
better transportation to carry increasing quantities
of goods. A third factor was the difficulty experienced
by the company in recruiting crews to row and track
York boats up the river systems of the new Canadian
Northwest.

On the Red River a steamboat had been in operation as early as 1859. The famous **International** was
put into commission in 1862. More steamboats did
not appear on the river until after 1872, the year the
Northern Pacific Railway reached Moorhead from

Duluth. With the completion of the railway, goods from Eastern Canada could be transported across the Great Lakes, sent in bond through American territory to Moorhead, and brought down the Red River to Fort Garry by riverboat. As soon as the railway was opened, trade on the river developed rapidly and more steamers were built in the next few years to carry freight and immigrants.[1]

The shareholders of the Hudson's Bay Company had been told by Governor Sir Stafford Henry Northcote in June, 1871, of the projected new method of transportation. Instead of sending goods by sea to York Factory, North America's "nearly completed railway system" would be utilized to give the Company a "very much shorter route." Where possible, the brigades of York boats would be replaced by steamers. At the November meeting of the shareholders, the Governor announced that two steamers had been ordered; one for use on Lake Winnipeg and one for the Saskatchewan River.

Some persons, during the decade of the 1870's advocated that boat connections with the Saskatchewan River from Winnipeg should be via lakes Manitoba and Winnipegosis rather than across Lake Winnipeg. One of these advocates was Donald A. Smith. As he expounded the scheme in the House of Commons, the Manitoba-Winnipegosis route would require but three short canals.[2] The first would cut across from the Assiniboine River at Poplar Point to Lake Manitoba. The second, at Meadow Portage between the two lakes, would need to be only three-eighths of a mile in length. At the northern end of

14

Lake Winnipegosis a four-mile canal across Mossy Portage would let boats out on Cedar Lake on the Saskatchewan, above the insurmountable barrier of Grand Rapids. An examination of the route by a Government survey in 1873[3] showed that canal construction would not be so simple as proponents of the route supposed. Since the elevation above sea level of the different bodies of water varied, locks would be required on the canals; further, the cutting of the canals across the necks of land would involve the moving of a greater yardage of earth than realized by the supporters of the route. The report either went unread or was ignored, for the route was still being promoted at the end of the decade.

The advocates of the lakes Manitoba-Winnipegosis route presented three arguments in its favor. With the building of the three canals, cargo might be carried on the same boat without transshipment from Winnipeg to Edmonton; (although the waters of the two lakes were calmer than those of Lake Winnipeg, it is doubtful if the keel-less riverboats would have survived even a breeze on such a wide expanse of water). A second argument was that the route would cut at least a hundred miles off the voyage to Edmonton. The third and most convincing argument was that the two lakes were clear of ice from two to four weeks earlier than the northern end of Lake Winnipeg, and the proposed route would lengthen the navigation season.

The lake steamer to which Governor Northcote had made reference was constructed at Lower Fort Garry during the winter of 1871-72. The builder was

Geological Survey of Canada

Lower Fort Garry The COLVILE *is moored beside a floating dock and warehouse constructed from the hull of the first lake steamer, the* CHIEF COMMISSIONER.

D. W. Hewitt. A one-funnel screw steamer, she was launched on May 7, 1872. Miss Mary Flett broke the traditional bottle of wine over her bow and christened her the **Chief Commissioner.**[4] This name was in honor of Donald A. Smith, at that time the holder of the office, and as such the person initiating the changes in transportation methods.

One tradition has it that the new vessel was intended to sail Lake Manitoba rather than Lake Winnipeg. At some time during the navigation season she tried to reach the former from Lake Winnipeg by way of the Dauphin River (at that time called the Little Saskatchewan), but the river was too shallow. Unable to get through, the **Chief Commissioner** was doomed to sail the rough waters of Lake Winnipeg, for which

16

she was ill-suited. Several years later the 1,200 cords of wood which had been cut and piled ready to fuel her furnaces might still be seen along her intended route.[5]

One of her earliest cargoes carried across Lake Winnipeg was materials for the building of a stern-wheel steamer for the Saskatchewan River.

In the first half of the 1870's, Winnipeg was conscious of its new ascendancy as the commercial import and export center of the Canadian Northwest.

The **Manitoba Daily Free Press** said editorially:
Not the least of the advantages which Winnipeg possesses in a commercial way is the fact of it being the principal centre of the fur trade of the North West. The proportion of the trade centering here will be greatly increased in the near future by the opening up of stage and steamboat lines through the interior.[6]

The Hudson's Bay Company, now assured of easier transportation of goods into the Northwest through Winnipeg, practically ceased to import through York Factory on Hudson Bay after 1874-75.

Chapter 4

FIRST STEAMBOAT

THE CONSTRUCTION of the new Saskatchewan steamer began early in 1873, above Grand Rapids. Built of lumber milled in Minnesota, she was to measure 142 feet in length with a 22-foot beam. Her two horizontal, high-pressure engines were by C. J. Dymont of Cincinnati. The builder was the same D. W. Hewitt who had built the **Chief Commissioner** the previous year.

The excitement and the anxiety of placing a steamboat on the Saskatchewan are preserved in a letter written at Grand Rapids by Inspecting Chief Factor Robert Hamilton five days before the boat sailed on her maiden voyage.[1] The Hudson's Bay Company had given Hamilton general supervision of the venture.

He described how he had waited anxiously at Fort Garry for word of the completion and trial run of the new steamer:

. . . Mr. McTavish was then in daily expectation of hearing from the Grand Rapids as to whether the steamer was a success or not for Hewitt, the

Builder, had been instructed before leaving the place to take her up as far as Cedar Lake. After waiting most anxiously for more than a fortnight Hewitt arrived at Fort Garry and told us that owing to the want of some iron for hanging his Rudder the trial could not be made, but that he felt perfectly confident the Boat would steam up with ease the Roches Rouge and Cross Lake Rapids. From other sources however I learned that the Boat was far from being a good one and that it was very doubtful if she would get up these Rapids.

Factor Hamilton, charged with the forwarding of the Company's fall outfit to Western and Northern posts, was concerned lest the boat fail:

And I therefore strongly urged Mr. McTavish to adhere to the original plan and send the outfit proper across land and send by steamer merely such supplies as would not affect our business provided the steamer should prove a failure; on his assurance however that even if the River Boat could not take up all the Saskat'n outfit there would still be plenty of time on returning it again to Red River to have it forwarded by carts, I gave an unwilling assent, but so that there might be no loss of time in getting it across the Portage here, I determined on coming out with the Propeller myself . . .

Inspecting Chief Factor Hamilton then described the trial run of the new vessel up-river a few miles:

A few days after I reached here Capt. Aymond got the necessary iron work arranged and we

19

made a trial trip of the new Boat. The water in the river is exceedingly high and in consequence the current is very strong, but we ran up it pretty well until it came to the very strongest part of the Roches Rouge when a strong head wind sprang up and we could make nothing of it. I feel assured however that if it had been calm the steamer would have run up. Andy Flavell the guide says if the boat can go up the Red Roche there is no other Rapid will stop her. Even if she cannot steam up she can always be taken up with a tow line attached to the small engine in her bow. The boat is not at all such as Hewitt the Builder undertook to construct. He gave an assurance that she would run at least twelve (12) miles an hour and we did not get more than seven and a half out of her the other day, altho those who pretend to know something about steamboating say that after a time when all is in fair working order she will run a mile or two faster per hour.

Such was the haste in getting the steamer into service in order that the fall supplies and trade goods would reach their destinations that the ship sailed unchristened and without ceremony. Anyone familiar with the superstitions associated with ships would have known that she would come to a bad end.

The captain of the unnamed boat was Frank (probably François) Aymond, who was to be in command on the Saskatchewan for four successive years. Born in St. Louis of French parentage, Aymond had been a riverman for many years. His name was long associated with the **Jeannette Roberts,** a Minnesota River boat, and from 1864 to 1871 with the **International** on the Red River. He was to spend four seasons on the Saskatchewan River.[2]

On August 2, the unnamed vessel sailed. She mounted the first rapid, Roche Rouge, with its "long gradual slope, with a deep channel of rolling, but comparatively unbroken water in the middle." A mile and a half beyond, at the exit from Cross Lake, were the rapids of the same name. The boat got up these small rapids, but she came to grief in the next rapids, only thirteen miles from her starting point.

In the Demi-Charge Rapids, so called because the York boats were tracked up with half cargoes, the river fell four feet in three-quarters of a mile. Two islands divided the river into three channels. Captain Aymond found the water unusually high and swift in the north channel, and tried another. The steam pressure in the vessel's boilers was pushed up to 145 pounds to the square inch, but she could not breast the current, and had to be warped up.

The difficulty of working steamers up the Demi-Charge was described some years later in a newspaper account:

> . . . a heavy piece of water, which it often takes the steamer a full day to ascend, the rope used being a mile and a quarter in length, having to be carried across a lake at the head of the rapids and fastened to trees on the opposite shore.[3]

On the forenoon of August 5, the boat had got up to the head of the Demi-Charge when she forged slightly ahead on her cable and taking a sudden sheer,

Public Archives of Canada

Demi-Charge Rapids

Demi-Charge Rapids—looking down to Cross Lake

came to rest on a rocky shoal. The wood of the hull being green and soft, and her cargo heavy, the weight of the boat as she settled on the rock crushed in a portion of her hull.[4]

22

Hamilton took charge of salvage operations, and by great exertion a considerable part of the cargo, consisting of dry goods and hardware, was saved. There were 200 kegs of sugar aboard; some of it was saved by boiling and evaporating over camp fires. The dry goods included the yearly dressmaking requirements of all the Indian women from The Pas to Hudson Hope. The bolts of cloth were spread out to dry on the trees and bushes of one of the islands, and to this day it is known as Calico Island.[5]

Hamilton sent off to The Pas and Cumberland House, asking that available canoemen come to the wreck with boats to help carry the goods inland as far as Fort Defiance. Henry Budd, the native catechist of the Church Missionary Society at The Pas, recorded in his diary that all able-bodied men had gone off to the wreck.[6]

In Winnipeg, the **Manitoban** reported, on October 11, that provisions and goods of every description were scarce in the upper Saskatchewan country, partly because of the loss of the steamer and the failure to get her cargo into the country. The Hudson's Bay Company, late in the season, dispatched trains of carts from Red River with much-needed supplies.

As for the boat, her stove-in hull was repaired sufficiently to get her back down to below the Roche Rouge Rapids, where she was seen later that season by a Geological Survey of Canada party headed by Alfred R. C. Selwyn.[7]

Selwyn was of the opinion that the construction of the boat made her unfit for service on the Saskatchewan:

Hudson's Bay Company Library

The NORTHCOTE at Cumberland House in 1894, some years after she was beached.

She was far too long and too weak both in hull and machinery, and when I saw her lying a wreck on the bank of the river, at the head of the Grand Rapid, I felt convinced that the man who built her could never have traversed the route for which she was designed, and I subsequently learnt that this was actually the case.[8]

In London, on November 25, a meeting of shareholders of the Hudson's Bay Company was informed of the loss of the steamer; the report said its destruction had been a disappointment, "as the difficulties of obtaining transport by the old methods are gradually increasing."

Chapter 5

S. S. NORTHCOTE

I N THE SUMMER of 1874, the ring of hammers could be heard early and late above Grand Rapids as work proceeded on a new river steamer and a barge. Most of the timber had been milled during the winter at Grand Forks, North Dakota. Construction was directed by an experienced boat builder, Captain J. Reeves, of that river town. The shipwrights were recruited in St. Paul through the good offices of N. W. Kittson.[1]

The new sternwheeler was a prototype of steamboats to be seen on the Mississippi and Missouri rivers, with her forecastle cut down to her main or boiler deck, two tall smokestacks well forward, and the pilot house behind them on the hurricane deck. Her hull was built entirely of Minnesota oak. She was 150 feet from bow to stern, 28.5 feet in breadth, and 4.5 feet deep. Her engines, salvaged from the unnamed boat, were capable of generating 39.72 horsepower. Her gross tonnage was 461.34, while her registered tonnage was 290.63.[2] With a light cargo her draft was 22 inches, but with a load of 150 tons she

From Hind, H. Y.: Red River and Saskatchewan exploring expeditions
*The Pas with Christ Church, and schoolhouse adjoining
church, 1858.*

drew 3.5 feet of water. Her capital value (in 1875) was $52,721.36.

The steamer was launched August 1 and duly christened the **Northcote** in honor of Sir Stafford Henry Northcote, later Earl of Iddesleigh, who was Governor of the Hudson's Bay Company from March, 1869, to March, 1874. It was he who presided over the meeting at which the Company agreed to sell Rupert's Land to the Dominion of Canada.

The S. S. **Northcote** sailed the third week of August, Captain Frank Aymond in command. The steamer's first port of call was The Pas, 140 miles upstream.

The Pas, situated on the south bank, was a Church of England missionary station. The white church with its tall spire (taken down a decade later when it became unsafe) would be the first sign to a boat of the nearness of a settlement. The church had been constructed between 1847 and 1857, and with the parsonage and schoolhouse, was the focal point of a scattered Indian village of some thirty or forty dwellings. Some land was under cultivation in and around the village.

In his journal, the Reverend Henry Budd noted with enthusiasm the steamboat's arrival:

August 26, 1874—The long expected steamer "North-Cote" [sic] came puffing up in sight. They blew the whistle so loud they made the very cattle rear up their heels, and took to full gallop with their tails up in the air in full speed to the woods. But, not only the cattle but the people of all ages and sexes were no less excited at the sight of the boat, the first boat of the kind to be seen by them all their life; in fact, the first steam boat going in this river since the Creation.[3]

Four days later the Sunday peace of the Indian settlement at Nepowewin Mission, across the river from Fort à la Corne and 240 miles above The Pas, was shattered by the whistle of the steamboat. The native catechist, Benjamin Constant, wrote in his journal of the arrival of the steamer in the afternoon and the cancellation of the evening service because the congregation was down looking at the new wonder.[4]

Twelve days out from Grand Rapids, the **Northcote** reached her destination, Carlton House, nearly 490 miles up-river. The captain decided it was inexpedient to proceed farther as the water was unusually low.[5]

Carlton House was square in layout, surrounded by a palisade nearly twenty feet high, strengthened by a bastion tower at each corner. On the inside of the palisade a gallery ran the length of the fort, from which defenders might fire their weapons. Since the fort was located on river-bottom land, and the bench-land behind was only a few hundred yards distant, a hypothetical enemy might have fired at ease into the enclosure from the higher ground. During much of the steamboat era the big house was occupied by Chief Factor Laurence Clarke. Sam B. Steele, who in 1874 was a member of "A" Division of the North West Mounted Police, which remained a week at Carlton House en route for Fort Saskatchewan, wrote of the post as follows:

> Here perfect discipline existed. The offices and stores were neat, and over each door was painted in French and English the names of the store and office, together with the class of goods in the buildings.[6]

From Greene, D. L.:
Christ Church, The Pas

Henry Budd, Indian clergyman who described the first call of the NORTHCOTE *in his diary.*

Canadian Illustrated News, April 21, 1877—Public Archives of Canada

Carlton House. Note the steamer NORTHCOTE on the river.

The fall outfits for the Northern posts in the Mackenzie River drainage system were brought up the Saskatchewan to this post, and from thence dispatched overland as far as the Churchill River · at Ile-à-la-Crosse, eventually reaching Fort McMurray on the Athabasca River. For some years the outfits continued to be dispatched from Carlton, but later these were shipped up the Saskatchewan to Fort Edmonton.

Chief Factor Alex Matheson, writing from The Pas, had this to say about the **Northcote's** return voyage:

She came back from Carlton all safe, though experiencing much more difficulty coming down stream than in going up. It is a delicate task to steer a huge leviathan like the Northcote in stony, crooked rapids, and it is the opinion of those who pretend to have some knowledge of the subject that there can't be certainty of final success until some boulders or other obstacles in the Nepowin and Coal Falls Rapids [sic] are moved. The steamer is now in winter quarters at Grand Rapids with the captain watching her, and putting up buildings for warehouse purposes at each end of the portage.[7]

Meantime the news of the first successful voyage up the Saskatchewan River had reached the outside world, and drew this optimistic forecast from the **St. Paul Press**:

Some years ago the press was accustomed to enlarge on the prospect of navigation from Breckenridge or Georgetown on the Red in this state

[Minnesota], through Lake Winnipeg and the North Saskatchewan to Fort Edmonton at the foot of the Rocky Mountains. . . . The steamboat just launched on the Saskatchewan is the forerunner of a great fleet of steam craft which is hereafter to navigate this long line of waterways.[8]

Chapter 6

NAVIGATION SEASONS 1875 AND 1876

I N THE 1875 navigational season, Captain Aymond was again master of the **Northcote.**
The new steamboat made one voyage upstream from Grand Rapids to Edmonton, and a
second one as far as Carlton House.

On the first trip of the season the **Northcote,**
after a voyage of eighteen days, reached Fort Edmonton on July 22, with a cargo estimated at 130 tons.
Her freight had left Lower Fort Garry only thirty-
four days before; fast transportation had come to the
Saskatchewan country.

The first voyage up-river above Carlton House
was described in a letter written by Inspecting Chief
Factor Hamilton from the latter place:

It took four days from this place to Fort Pitt
and from there to Edmonton four days. As far
as Fort Pitt we were in places rather troubled
with sand bars but nothing to cause any anxious
delay, and from thence to our destination we
found no obstruction, but a stronger current in
the River. On our downward passage we were only
three days and a half including all stoppages.[1]

The letter continues with a description of the second time the sternwheeler descended the Cole's Falls series of rapids:

As the cargo shipped from this place to Grand Rapid was a very valuable one [furs] and the Captain of the Boat being very nervous about the Coles [sic] Falls I thought it better to accompany the Boat as far as the Forks which I accordingly did and saw her safely past all danger on the morning of the 1st Inst. We went down the Coles Falls in glorious style in rather less than one hour. The water was in very fair stage but not what could be called high. If our brilliant government would expend a little money on the improvement of the Saskatchewan navigation they would confer a benefit on the country and it would not take much to remove from the channel some of the large Boulder stones which at present makes the Coles Falls a dangerous place to run down when the water is at all low.

Arriving back at Grand Rapids, the **Northcote** had to tie up for a month to await the arrival of more cargo from Lower Fort Garry. A new lake steamer was under construction, and the delay in getting her into service affected transportation along the Saskatchewan.[2]

The **Chief Commissioner** having been found unsatisfactory for the rough waters of Lake Winnipeg, the Hudson's Bay Company ordered a new lake steamer built at Grand Forks, North Dakota. Captain Reeves was her builder. She was to have been ready to operate by the time the ice went out on the north-

Geological Survey of Canada

The Hudson's Bay Company post at Grand Rapids in 1890.

ern end of the lake, about the end of June, but her hull did not reach Lower Fort Garry until July 16. The engines for the new vessel were taken from the **Chief Commissioner,** whose hull was then converted into a floating warehouse. The new steamer was a one-deck caravel-type vessel with a gross tonnage of 164.41. Christened the S.S. **Colvile,** she was destined to ply the waters of Lake Winnipeg for nineteen seasons until destroyed by fire on Sunday morning, July 15, 1894, while lying at the wharf below Grand Rapids.

On her maiden voyage the **Colvile** did not reach Grand Rapids until September 3. By then, the waters of the Saskatchewan were so low that the **Northcote** was fortunate to get upstream as far as Carlton. The delay made it necessary for James A. Grahame, now Chief Commissioner of the Company, to hire four

35

hundred carts to move the Western outfits across land from Carlton. Writing from Fort Edmonton on Christmas Eve, Inspecting Chief Factor Hamilton commented:

The residue of the outfit for the post of Edmonton will cost a big amount for freight up from Carlton at this season, as men cannot be induced to travel under double the usual freight price.[3]

The **Northcote** was run into the mouth of the Sturgeon River, five miles west of Prince Albert, for the winter. Captain Aymond and his family also went into winter quarters in the settlement.

Prince Albert had been founded in 1866 when the Rev. James Nisbet, a Presbyterian clergyman from Kildonan on the Red River, had arrived to found an Indian mission. Each year had brought more settlers from the clergyman's former parish, and these had been joined by Hudson's Bay Company officials upon retirement from the service. In 1874, the Prince Albert settlement straggled along the south bank of the river for four or five miles. Agriculture was still limited in extent, but in the first years of the steamboat era would expand rapidly. Within a few years, lumber and grist mills would be established.

The Saskatchewan River, in the 1876 navigation season, was in low stage during much of the summer, and consequently little was accomplished by the steamer.

The **Northcote** left her winter berth in May, and went up-river to Edmonton carrying the cargo she had disembarked the previous fall at Carlton House. On her return voyage she had to contend with low water. Carrying a fair cargo of furs, the steamboat left Carlton on June 4, reaching Grand Rapids five days later. Here she had to tie up until the arrival of the **Colvile.**

The river steamer sailed on June 27, bound for Carlton. Incomplete evidence suggests that she was unable to climb Cole's Falls, as Chief Commissioner Grahame, while visiting Grand Rapids, was in receipt of a report that Captain Aymond and Pilot Joseph Favell had absolutely refused to attempt the ascent. The boat was said to be drawing seventeen inches of water, and although there were three feet on the Falls, the channel was too crooked and boulder-strewn to risk her.[4]

The **Northcote** departed Grand Rapids a second time on August 8. She made slow progress, for Cumberland House was not reached until eight days later and the bottom of Thorburn Rapids on August 19. These rapids were climbed only with great difficulty after fifty tons of cargo had been unloaded on the bank. Reaching Cole's Falls, she was again unable to ascend them and had to unload the remaining hundred tons of freight. The freight was later forwarded by cart, at much greater expense.

On the return voyage the sternwheeler picked up the cargo left at Thorburn Rapids and arrived back at Grand Rapids on September 28. The boat wintered at the upper end of Cedar Lake.[5]

Captain Aymond was dismissed at the end of the season as master of the **Northcote.**[6] Not only were Company officials dissatisfied with his management of the vessel, but the pilot and engineers had refused to again serve under him.

The termination of the captain's services gives credence to a tale of mutiny found in the reminiscences of a Company official writing under his Indian sobriquet, O-ge-mas-es (Little Clerk).[7] According to the writer, the captain was much given to strange oaths and wild rages, and these antagonized the Indian stevedores and other crew members.

On the occasion of the mutiny, the **Northcote** had set off upstream from Grand Rapids. On the evening of the day following, a canoe arrived at Grand Rapids from Cedar Lake with a message from the captain saying that the boat was tied up by a strike. O-ge-mas-es was sent by canoe to mediate the differences between the captain and his crew.

At Chemahawin, O-ge-mas-es found the captain in a fine rage aboard ship, while the crew loafed on the bank. The mediator coaxed the captain to his cabin, told him to remain there until the difficulty was settled, and warned him that he might lose his job if the steamer did not get under way before the river fell too low for her to proceed. O-ge-mas-es met the malcontents, shook hands all around, joked with the men, and ordered the steward to prepare the best meal possible. Afterwards, O-ge-mas-es challenged the ringleader to take half the crew and see which team could unload the most freight. The challenge was accepted, and the unloading of cargo and the loading of cordwood for fuel were carried out in record time. When the boat sailed, the captain was warned to stay out of the way of the crew as much as possible. As described earlier, the boat got only as far as the foot of Cole's Falls.

Captain Aymond is said to have retired to a farm four miles above Neche on the Pembina River in Dakota Territory, where he died some years later.

Chapter 7

NAVIGATION SEASON 1877

THE YEAR 1877 was a banner year for steam navigation on the Saskatchewan. A new steamboat company was incorporated, and although nothing came of it, its formation indicated that entrepreneurs saw possibilities in the expanding trade of the Saskatchewan country. Regular inspection of steamboats also reached the Saskatchewan. A tramway was built around Grand Rapids. A new steamboat, the **Lily,** was assembled above Grand Rapids. And finally, the **Northcote** had the most profitable season she would ever experience, six successful voyages upstream.

The Saskatchewan Transportation and Trading Company Limited was incorporated in April. The Company's prospectus envisaged two boats on the lakes Manitoba-Winnipegosis route and two more on the Saskatchewan River, with bimonthly trips from Winnipeg to Edmonton.[1] An undated memorial to the Dominion Government asked for a subsidy of $50,000 for ten years, in return for which the Company would carry the mails free. As the Government did not see

Public Archives of Canada

Grand Rapids portage.

41

fit to grant the subsidy, the Company's plans came to naught.

The first inspector of steamboats for the Manitoba, Keewatin, and North West Division of the Department of Marine was appointed on February 2. Edmund R. Abell was an American, born April 11, 1826. He was a steamboat engineer from Minnesota who had been in charge of the installation of the engines in the **International,** the Red River's second sternwheeler, in 1861. He was engineer on the lake steamer **Chief Commissioner** in the 1874 season. In his new capacity, he arrived at Grand Rapids where he inspected the **Northcote** for the first time on August 28.[2]

During the summer the Hudson's Bay Company constructed a tramway around Grand Rapids to expedite the transshipment of goods from lake steamers to river steamers. In 1872 the Company had surveyed land at either end of the Rapids, obtaining title to two plots of fifty acres each. After the **Northcote** had been put into service it was found that the wharf on the upper plot was dangerously close to the Rapids for the safety of the vessel. The Company submitted a request to the Department of the Interior asking that the plot and wharf be relocated. Instead, the Department gave the Company a third tract of eight acres of land on which to locate its upper wharf and warehouse.

At the same time, in 1876, the Company negotiated for a fifty-foot wide right of way for a tramway from below to above the Rapids. The Government gave the Company a twenty-one year lease in return for rental of ten dollars per annum.[3] Over a hundred tons of iron rails and four tramcars were brought to the site aboard the **Colvile** in the summer of 1877. The narrow-gauge line was about three and one-half miles long, and was said to have cost over twenty thousand dollars.[4] A tramcar could carry three tons, and one horse could draw three cars. The upper and lower ends of the tramway were connected later by telephone.

Construction was directed by Walter Moberly, under contract. Moberly was a distinguished civil engineer, with considerable experience in railway construction. In British Columbia, he had surveyed much of the route east of the Fraser Canyon later followed by the Canadian Pacific Railway. He had discovered Eagle Pass in 1865. In the 1870's, he was chief engineer for the Manitoba South-Western Railway. Another of his achievements was the construction of the first system of sewers of the city of Winnipeg.[5]

The new tramway was opened on September 11 by the Governor General of Canada, the Marquis of Dufferin, and Lady Dufferin, who were paying an official visit to Manitoba and Keewatin. The Marchioness later described their arrival aboard the **Colvile** at the wharf below the Rapids:

> There is not very much to see at this particular spot: trees on each side of the river, two large wooden houses at the wharf, and some groups of Indians sitting about. They had put up decorations, and fired off their guns as usual. Mr. McTavish, one of the Hudson's Bay Company, came to meet us, and took us two miles across

Glenbow Foundation

The LILY *under construction at Yarrow & Co., Glasgow.*

the portage on a tramway laid down since July, and the first railway in the North-West. The car was most gorgeously lined with coloured blankets, and when we got out of it we jumped into spring-carts, in which we did the unfinished part of the railway. During the drive we saw some views of the river, and went to the Hudson's Bay Company store. We then inspected a new steel steamer, and lunched; and I put in a rivet in the last bit of the railway, and was presented with the hammer.[6]

Walter Moberly recalled, in his memoirs, that in the construction camp the men had managed to make a spike and hammer out of steel, and had polished them till they looked like silver. He had "thought of appropriating [the hammer] as a memento of the occasion," but the Marchioness had kept it.[7]

The new steamboat above Grand Rapids inspected by the vice-regal party was the S. S. **Lily.**

44

She was built for the Hudson's Bay Company at a cost of £4,010 in the Clyde shipyards of Yarrow and Company, a firm which built similar boats for the rivers of Brazil and central Africa. She was shipped out from England in sections in the summer of 1876,[8] and reassembled under the direction of two English machinists, Messrs. Bodden and Tobbin,[9] who came out in 1877.

The **Lily** was a two-decked sternwheeler, 100 feet in length and 24 feet in the beam, with a depth of 4 feet. She had a draft of 14 inches, even keel, which was 4 inches more than intended. The boat's machinery included a loco-boiler, and two 13-inch cylinders with a stroke of 36 inches. Her engine power was 31.80 horsepower and her gross tonnage was 207.01.[10] The most notable feature about her was that she had a steel hull, steam and exhaust pipes of copper, and a brass-fitted engine.[11] Unfortunately, the steel plates of her hull were easily damaged on rocks in the river.

The **Lily** sailed for Prince Albert with a cargo of twenty tons, the 1878 outfits for the Athabasca and Mackenzie districts.[12] As she was unable to get above Cumberland House because of the low stage of the water, she discharged her cargo and returned to Grand Rapids. Captain John Griggs, who commanded the **Northcote** that season, took charge of the **Lily** for her maiden voyage. Though not successful in proceeding very far up-river, she had demonstrated that she was the speediest craft on prairie waters.

The intention of the Company was to employ the new vessel on the upper portion of the river between Carlton House and Fort Edmonton, while the **Northcote** would carry cargo on the lower river as far as Carlton.[13]

Captain Griggs, who was on the Saskatchewan for his first season, would be in command of the **Northcote** for three more seasons before his death during the winter of 1880-81. He had originally been on the Minnesota River, but had spent some years on the Red River, and made his home at Grand Forks.

At the beginning of the 1877 season, the **Northcote** had left her winter quarters at Chemahawin on May 4. On her first voyage, she reached Edmonton on May 29. She made four more voyages to Carlton House, and a sixth voyage as far as Cumberland House. Her season ended when she came down to the head of the Demi-Charge Rapids on September 4.[14]

Passenger traffic on the Saskatchewan was increasing. In the report on the operation of the **Northcote** for the 1877 season made to the London office, the proposal was put forth that the cabin which provided accommodation only for crew should be expanded for the carrying of passengers. The number of applications for passage on the vessel had increased that season.[15] When the alteration of the steamer was made, is not known, but some years later the **Northcote** is described as having accommodation for fifty passengers.

Chapter 8

NAVIGATION SEASON 1878

THE NAVIGATION SEASON of 1878, like that of 1876, was one of low water in the river and of hazard and frustration for the two steamboats. In the spring the water was in such low stage that the **Northcote** could not descend the Demi-Charge, Cross Lake, and Roche Rouge rapids from her winter quarters on Cedar Lake to Grand Rapids until June 27. She was detained three days at Grand Rapids awaiting a further rise in the water level. She then had a successful voyage up to Carlton. She arrived back at Grand Rapids on July 22, loaded cargo, and set off again, accompanied by the **Lily,** three days later. The two boats reached their destination, Carlton, on August 7.[1]

The **Northcote,** on her return voyage downstream, suffered damage while descending the crooked, boulder-strewn rapids of Cole's Falls.

The steamer Northcote on August 17 struck a sunken rock running the Coles Falls on the Saskatchewan River. The vessel struck upon the starboard quarter forward and across to the port side about two-thirds of her length breaking eighty-three frames, and damaging her planking.[2]

CFRN-TV, Edmonton

The rapids on the lower Saskatchewan on the Sturgeon-Weir route photographed about 1925.

The company shareholders were told that "by the judicious care on the part of the officers the cargo on board was brought to its destination in a satisfactory condition."[3]

The **Lily** did not sail from Grand Rapids until July 25, as her engineers were busy making adjustments to her machinery. She apparently had not been equipped with a proper machine-operated capstan which was so necessary in working the vessel up rapids. The new capstan installed was too light and broke at her first test in the Roche Rouge, and again next day in the Demi-Charge. Fortunately, the **Lily** was accompanied by the **Northcote,** which gave the new steel vessel assistance in climbing the rapids. The absence of water heaters was another serious defect, since the constant influx of cold water affected everything it came in touch with, particularly the boiler flues, which kept springing leaks.[4]

Chief Factor Alex Matheson, of The Pas, wrote with some feeling from Carlton about the Lily's upward passage:

By the blessing of Providence we managed to get the Lily here at last, and now she is with all her responsibilitv on the hands of Mr. Clarke, and I sincerely wish him more joy of her than I have had.

We got along from Cumberland all right, at least so far as the rapids were concerned, for we only had to warp over two of the Coles' Falls [sic], and then by hand as our capstan's steam gear was broken.

The Northcote is here yet, but will be leaving tomorrow if the water continues to fall. All hands are busy digging a site for the Lily to be hauled out on making . . . capstans . . .[5]

Hundreds of carts and countless swarms of people are about this place at this time, & Mr. Clarke has his hands pretty full, some are sent to Green Lake, some to Edmonton and they are both going & coming all the time. Steamboating is expensive no doubt but whatever may be said, it can be no more than a fleabite to cart transport.

I return from here as soon as the Lily is hauled out, which won't be yet for some time.[6]

Chapter 9

NAVIGATION SEASON 1879

T HE **NORTHCOTE** after undergoing repairs
to the damage caused in Cole's Falls the previous year, made two voyages up to Prince
Albert and Carlton in June and July of 1879. On
her third voyage the passengers and cargo had signi-
ficance for the Indian population along the Saskatchewan. Aboard were several farm instructors assigned to Indian reserves, and agricultural equipment,
seed, and livestock to introduce the Indians to farm-
ing. These were being supplied by the Dominion
Government in fulfillment of commitments undertaken in Treaty No. 6, signed three years earlier at
Carlton and Fort Pitt.

On this voyage the water was in low stage, and
the heavily laden vessel had to spar herself over many
shoals. As she was straining over one of these the
capstan broke into fragments, knocking the second
engineer senseless and seriously injuring him. The
Demi-Charge Rapids on the lower river and the
Thorburn Rapids further up were ascended only
with difficulty.[1] When the steamboat reached the
Forks, the officers informed Chief Factor Laurence

Clarke, who met the vessel, that Cole's Falls could not be climbed.

The fifty-two head of farm animals were landed and driven overland to the Muskoday Reserve, while the **Northcote** followed up the South Saskatchewan. Four days later, and after much labor sparring over shoals, she reached the reserve. Here, Chief Factor Clarke mobilized 150 carts, no doubt from the half-breed settlements along the river, to carry the freight to the depot at Carlton and to various Indian reserves.[2]

The **Northcote** was laid up for the season above Grand Rapids on September 12.[3]

Meanwhile, the **Lily,** operating on the North Saskatchewan out of Carlton and Prince Albert, had a successful season until she struck a rock below Fort Saskatchewan early in August.[4]

The new captain of the **Lily** was John H. Smith, who was later to make his home at Prince Albert for some years. In 1874 and 1875, on the Red River, he served as mate of the **Dakota** and **Selkirk** respectively. He is said to have helped build the lake steamer **Chief Commissioner,** and to have later been her captain, and subsequently captain of her successor, the **Colvile.** On the Saskatchewan River he would be in command of the **Lily** for three seasons, 1879-81, and after an absence of eight years, return as skipper of the **North West** for two of her last years of service, 1889 and 1890.[5]

Captain Smith arrived at Carlton by trail from Winnipeg on May 24 to take charge of his ship. Two days later the **Lily** sailed ˙for Prince Albert to pick up cargo. Upward bound she put in at Battleford on

June 2 to unload flour, and continued to the upper ports. She reached Edmonton on June 10, just nine days' and two hours' sailing from Carlton. At Edmonton, most of the cargo unloaded was Company goods for the Peace River country. The ship remained at Edmonton until June 25, awaiting the arrival of the winter's furs from the north country. She arrived in Battleford two days later. Sailing up the Battle River to the town for the first time, her jackstaff caught on the telegraph wires, pulling down wires and poles as far as the top of the hill.

On July 1 she was in Battleford again, with 900 bags of flour and other freight. Ten days later she returned on her third upward voyage, and stayed only long enough to discharge 15,992 pounds of freight for the Company's post. She continued up-river with the Company's outfit of trade goods for the West.

The **Lily's** next voyage was a memorable one. Aboard were Lieutenant-Governor Laird of the Northwest Territories with his secretary, A. E. Forget, and Mrs. Forget, paying an official visit to the upper Saskatchewan country. Also aboard was stipendiary magistrate Colonel Richardson, going to Fort Saskatchewan police barracks to try a case of cannibalism by an Indian accused of eating his wife and children during the previous hard winter.

The upward voyage was uneventful, except for sparring the steamer over a few sand bars, the skipper shooting a bear swimming in the water, and official welcomes for the vice-regal party at each river port. On the morning of August 5 the **Lily,** gaily decked with bunting, came in view of the Hudson's Bay

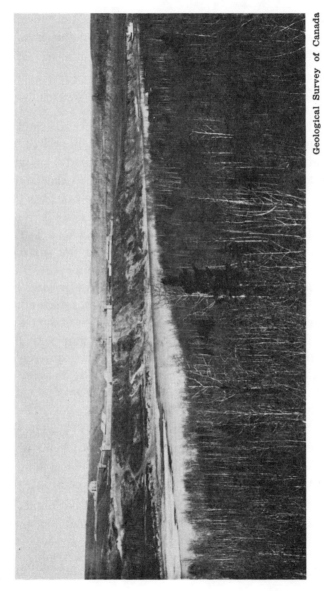

Geological Survey of Canada

Fort Edmonton from the south bank of the Saskatchewan River. Note the LILY beached for the winter after being brought back up-river after her disaster, September, 1879.

Company's Fort Edmonton. Flags flew from the fort, and two ancient pieces of ordnance on the grass outside the stockade fired an official salute.

The fort stood on the high bank above the river, the usual stockaded post with corner bastions. A little to the east, a couple of warehouses stood apart but surrounded by a lower stockade. Farther up the slope was Chief Factor Hardisty's big house, built five years earlier outside the security of the palisades to signify that peace and civilization had come to the frontier.

Early on August 7 the **Lily** steamed away from **Edmonton, and by nine o'clock was some ten miles** below Fort Saskatchewan. The morning was clear and pleasant with a slight breeze rippling the surface of the water. Both the captain and the pilot were in the wheelhouse when the steamer hit an underwater rock. When Captain Smith went below deck, he found that the steamer had struck near the center about twenty feet from the stern, and that the water was rising rapidly in the rear compartments. He ordered the boat run to the shore, and there tried to keep her afloat by holding her up with spars, but the stern gradually settled in eight feet of water.

Governor Laird sent back to Fort Saskatchewan for a skiff, and next morning the party set out to row to Battleford; an ignominious way in which to return from a voyage which had begun so ceremoniously!

When the **Lily** was raised, it was found that about four feet of her steel plates had been torn loose, leaving an opening of six inches. By September 18 temporary repairs enabled her to reach Edmonton, where she was put in winter berth.

The Hudson's Bay Company shareholders, at a meeting on July 6, 1880, were given the following information about the repairs to the steel steamer:

In consequence of the accident to the steamer "Lily", reported in November last, and difficulties attending the navigations of the River Saskatchewan, it has been found necessary to sanction the sheeting of that vessel, which will be attended to in the course of the present session.[6]

This work was done during the winter of 1880-81 at Prince Albert. The flat bottom of the steamer was sheeted with two-inch spruce planking, but "the extra weight and bulk made her so unwieldy as to be of very little use."[7]

An important decision about the water transport business was taken by the Council of the Hudson's Bay Company during its annual meeting held at Carlton House, July 5-16. The decision, as reported by the **Saskatchewan Herald,** was as follows:

The Company has decided as far as it possibly can be done without interference with its own business, to extend to the general public the facilities for travel and the transportation of freight offered by its lake and river steamers. The tariff of prices of merchandise has also been so regulated as to meet the growing demands of the custom trade of the country and the Company is further prepared to make special rates for customers who deal largely with it—whether traders or not—both in the sale of its goods, and in the purchase of the usual products of the country. These enlightened and progressive measures have received the full approval of the Chief Commissioner and the Council.[8]

The following January, correspondence passed between C. J. Brydges, Land Commissioner of the Hudson's Bay Company, and Sir Alexander Campbell, then Postmaster-General of Canada, about the rates for passengers and freight on the steamers. The Company agreed to reduce the rates on freight for Dominion Government departments, and also the rates charged the general public.[9]

A writer[10] in 1879 stated that a thousand tons was the lowest calculation of the freight carried into the Saskatchewan country and the further North by Red River carts alone each year, at an average cost of $200 per ton. The cart rate that year had ranged from $8.50 to $14.00 per hundredweight. The steamboat rates put into force the following season, 1880, show that the cost of shipping a hundredweight to Edmonton was only $6.25.

Chapter 10

NAVIGATION SEASON 1880

THE WEATHER in the summer and fall of 1880 was unusually wet, and consequently, the Saskatchewan River was in good stage for steamboat navigation. Late in August the water rose to flood level, an unusual occurrence for that season; a Mr. McKay, resident at Prince Albert, declared that in the sixty-three years he had lived beside the Saskatchewan, he had never before seen such high water in the autumn.[1] The high water extended the shipping season and was a great boon to those shipping goods into the country.

The Hudson's Bay Company published its new schedule of freight and passenger rates in Western newspapers early in the summer of 1880. In order to carry passengers, it was necessary to provide suitable accommodations on the steamers.[2]

The altered appearance of the lake steamer, the **Colvile,** was described in a Winnipeg newspaper:

The appearance of the steamer is somewhat changed by the recent addition of an upper cabin for the accommodation of a few passengers. There are in this cabin six state-rooms, three on

57

each side and a dining hall about 12 feet square. The structure is placed between the smokestack and the forward gangway, the new wheel house being at the forward end. Mr. D. B. Reeves of Grand Forks is the builder.[3]

Likewise, the cabin of the **Lily** was expanded. During the downward voyage from her winter berth at Edmonton, the ship's carpenter, James MacDonald, built an additional fifteen feet to the cabin for state-rooms.[4]

The **Northcote,** for some reason, did not sail from Grand Rapids until July 10. She towed a barge of machinery consigned to Edmonton. Thus encumbered, and breasting a strong current as the river was high, the sternwheeler's progress was slow. Meantime, at Carlton, Chief Factor Clarke, concerned when the steamer failed to appear, set off aboard the **Lily** on July 22 in search of her. She was found twenty miles below Fort à la Corne, making little headway against the heavy current. The **Lily** took off sixty tons of her cargo. The **Northcote's** little "nigger" had smashed, and unaided, she could not have climbed Cole's Falls. Even with the assistance of the **Lily,** it took her four days to climb the series of rapids. She docked at Prince Albert at two o'clock on the morning of July 29.[5]

An example of the frustrating delays experienced by shippers and travelers was that of Lieutenant-Governor Laird and his family, leaving the country via the Saskatchewan River. The family left Battleford on the **Lily** on July 5, expecting to connect promptly with the **Northcote,** but were detained three weeks at Prince Albert when she did not arrive on time.[6]

58

STEAMBOAT TARIFFS, 1880
FREIGHT RATES

Lower Fort Garry	Freight Per Pound	
	Up	Down
To Grand Rapids	1¼ cts.	1¼ cts.
The Pas	2½ cts.	2¼ cts.
Cumberland	2¾ cts.	2½ cts.
Fort à la Corne	3 cts.	2½ cts.
Prince Albert	3½ cts.	2½ cts.
Carlton	3¾ cts.	3 cts.
Battleford	4½ cts.	3½ cts.
Fort Pitt	5¼ cts.	4 cts.
Victoria	5¾ cts.	4½ cts.
Fort Saskatchewan	6¼ cts.	5 cts.
Edmonton	6¼ cts.	5 cts.

PASSENGER RATES

Lower Fort Garry	Up		Down	
	Cabin	Deck	Cabin	Deck
To Grand Rapids	$12.00	$ 5.00	$12.00	$ 5.00
The Pas	24.00	10.00	18.00	7.50
Cumberland	30.00	15.00	24.00	12.00
Fort à la Corne	35.00	20.00	35.00	20.00
Prince Albert	50.00	25.00	40.00	20.00
Carlton	50.00	25.00	40.00	20.00
Battleford	60.00	30.00	50.00	25.00
Fort Pitt	65.00	32.50	60.00	30.00
Victoria, Fort Saskatchewan, and Edmonton	70.00	35.00	65.00	32.00

Cabin passengers were entitled to a berth in the cabin but had to pay 50 cents for each meal. Deck passengers had to provide their own bedding and pay 50 cents per meal. Each passenger was allowed one hundred pounds of baggage free. Should the steamer be arrested en route through accident or other cause, passengers were expected to accomplish the remainder of the journey at their own cost and in the best way they could.

From Begg, Alexander: History of the North-West. pp. 338-39

Other passengers aboard the **Northcote** when she left for down-river on July 30 were Mr. and Mrs. Joseph Reader, missionaries sponsored by the Church Missionary Society, heading for a new posting at The Pas. The following day, their son was born aboard the steamboat near Cumberland House and fittingly christened Northcote Reader. This boy, probably the only baby ever born on a sternwheeler on the river, was to live for many years beside the Saskatchewan.[7]

The **Northcote** made four more voyages upstream. Her second voyage was to Carlton, her third to Prince Albert, her fourth to Cumberland House, and her fifth and last, in late September, as far as the Forks where low water prevented her proceeding further.

From Tuttle, C. R.: Our north land

A sketch of Fort à la Corne from a book by Charles Richard Tuttle entitled Our north land.

The **Lily** went upstream with six cargoes during the season, one trip as far as Battleford only, the others to Edmonton. Her inbound freight was mostly for the Company and for Dominion Government departments, particularly Indian Affairs. On her fourth trip she towed a barge containing machinery consigned to Edmonton, a steam gristmill for the Company, a sawmill for McLeod, Norris & Belcher. On a later voyage she carried a threshing machine to Edmonton, indicating the development of agricultural settlement. Thus, oats for livestock, wheat for milling, and lumber for building were exchanged between Edmonton, Battleford, and Prince Albert. On her last down voyage the **Lily** carried coal to be tried as winter fuel at Carlton House.

A dispatch from Edmonton which appeared in the **Saskatchewan Herald** on November 29 described the growth of trade in that center. The settlement boasted eight stores, besides that of the Hudson's Bay Company. In addition to the six cargoes landed by the **Lily,** over 300 cartloads of freight had arrived, and the Company still had a large train of carts bringing further goods up from Carlton.

At the end of the 1880 season the report on the steamboats laid before the Hudson's Bay Company's shareholders said:

> The steamers on Lake Winnipeg and the Saskatchewan have been fully employed during the past season in conveying the goods and returns of the Company to and from Fort Garry, and in carrying other supplies and passengers at satisfactory rates. In view of the increasing traffic on the Saskatchewan, the Committee has determined to build another steamer to assist the 'Northcote' and also to provide further communication on Lake Winnipeg by a supplemental vessel to the steamer 'Colvile', and they hope that these additional boats will be found equal to the task of meeting the demands expected to be made of them next season.[8]

From Winnipeg, C. J. Brydges, in a letter to the Honorable H. L. Langevin, Minister of Public Works, requested that the Dominion Government dredge the bar at the mouth of the Red River and remove certain obstacles to navigation on the Saskatchewan River, so that the Hudson's Bay Company might construct boats of larger capacity. The bar at the mouth of the Red River limited the draft of vessels going out on Lake Winnipeg to five or six feet. The Company wanted to construct a lake boat of greater draft, not only to carry more cargo but to navigate the lake better in rough weather.

With another boat on the lake, Brydges said, another riverboat would be needed:

. . . it will be necessary to put an additional steamer of large capacity on the Saskatchewan River; and we are prepared to build this boat, and have her ready for the next year's work, if we can have assurance that work necessary for her safe passage will be undertaken by the Government.[9]

The two steamers proposed for construction during the winter of 1880-81 would have given the Company a fleet of five steamers, two on Lake Winnipeg and three on the Saskatchewan River. With the enlarged fleet the Company might have offered reasonable regularity in the service and sufficient tonnage to meet the expanding freight and passenger business. The steamers would have represented an investment by the Company of approximately $100,000.

But we do not run the risk without the navigation is improved in the way Mr. Langevin knows all about. The risk is too serious at present.[10]

Since the Department of Public Works did not begin any of the improvements requested until 1882, the boats were not built.

Chapter 11

NAVIGATION SEASON 1881

THE TWO STEAMBOATS in service on the Saskatchewan were overhauled in the spring of 1881, the **Northcote** at Grand Rapids, the **Lily** at Prince Albert. The **Northcote** had some new machinery installed. The **Lily** was repaired, and her saloon "enlarged and elegantly fitted up"—according to a journalistic report of the day.

The **Winnipeg Daily Times,** on June 1, recorded the departure on the lake steamer **Colvile** of the officers of the two Saskatchewan steamboats. Captain John Smith was again in command of the iron boat. Captain Jerry Webber, a newcomer to the Saskatchewan River, was skipper of the **Northcote,** replacing Captain John Griggs, who had died during the winter.

Captain Webber[1] was a typical Mississippi riverman. From the time he ran away from home at the age of eleven to become a cabin boy on an Ohio packet until his death at eighty-six, he followed steamboating. He was born in 1822 at East Liverpool, Ohio. After moving to the upper Mississippi in 1851, he became one of the first captains on the Minnesota River.

Captain Webber's most memorable feat as a pilot was associated with the defence of the Union when the Civil War broke out early in 1861. The military wanted Sherman's battery of artillery moved from the isolated Indian post of Fort Ridgeley down to the lower Mississippi, where it could be used in defence against Confederacy incursions. The Minnesota River had one of the most twisted, crooked channels in the West, and in April, the river valley was in flood, in places a mile wide from bluff to bluff. The problem of navigating down the flooded river, with a strong current pushing, was to keep a boat in the channel. Captain Webber's boat, the **Fanny Harris,** loaded the battery and started down-river.

The captain would ring his bells for "reverse" as he rounded the countless points, but it was impossible in the current to back her or even to stop her. The best the engineers could do was to check her speed and let her drift round wooded points where trees and boughs would rake her whole length, tearing down stanchions, guards, and gingerbread work. The boat successfully won through to Fort Snelling, but she had suffered $2,000 worth of damage. Captain Webber was well-known among rivermen for this superb feat of piloting.

During the Civil War, while he was on the lower Mississippi, Captain Webber is said to have been captured by guerrillas, but to have escaped and made his way back to the Union lines. In the decade of the 1870's (except for 1877 when he was on the Missouri River), he was employed mostly on the Red River. There is a record of him on the **Selkirk** in

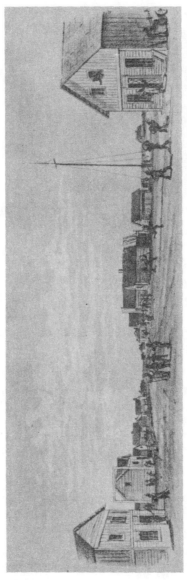

Public Archives of Canada

This sketch of Battleford shows it as it was in the 1880's when river transportation was active. The sketch is from the Canadian Pictorial & Illustrated War News, 1885, April 4 issue. The scene shows the street as it probably looked when the town was occupied by rebels and Indians, March 30, 1885. (See Chapters 23 and 24).

1871 and again in 1874, and on the **Dakota** for the two intervening seasons.

To return to navigation on the Saskatchewan in 1881, the **Winnipeg Daily Times,** on June 9, informed the public that passengers leaving on the next sailing of the **Colvile** could expect to make close connections at Grand Rapids with the **Lily** for all points on the Saskatchewan. The **Lily,** which had previously confined her voyaging to the north branch, was coming down to pick up freight and passengers, as the **Northcote** was still undergoing renovations.

Upward bound, the **Lily** put into Battleford on July 22, with seventy tons of freight, mainly for the Department of Indian Affairs. At this port she took on twenty tons for Edmonton, merchandise that had been carted overland from Winnipeg. On her way back down from Edmonton as far as Fort Pitt, the steamer experimented with coal as fuel, and found that she was able to maintain a steady steam pressure of a hundred pounds to the inch.

The **Lily** operated much later in the season than normally. She went upstream again in late August. On September 24 she arrived in Battleford with local freight for the Hudson's Bay Company, and also with the Fort Pitt outfit. On October 4, she was back with a cargo of oats for the horses of the North West Mounted Police.

During the 1881 season the **Northcote** appeared on the north branch above Carlton for the first time since 1877. The sternwheeler arrived in Battleford with a cargo of 180 tons on July 16, and came back down-river with lumber on July 25. She reached Grand

Sketch by S. Hall—Public Archives of Canada

Early visitors made good use of river navigation. Among them was the Marquis of Lorne, then Governor General. In this sketch by S. Hall Indians are sitting on the grass in Fort Carlton listening to speakers during his visit in 1881. (Mr. Hall was a newspaper correspondent traveling with the vice-regal party.)

Rapids four days later. On August 15 she was back at Battleford, Edmonton bound, with 160 tons of freight and some passengers. She passed Battleford on the return voyage on August 23, having made the round trip in less than eight days. At Carlton House she took aboard the Governor General, the Marquis of Lorne, and his party. The Governor General was making an official tour of the Northwest Territories.

Pageantry and barbaric splendor mingled when the vice-regal party with its escort of fifty red-coated Mounted Police came down into the river valley at Carlton House. Here were the brown, weather-beaten bastioned walls of the fort, and scattered over the valley the teepees of the natives. The following morning a council was held, the Governor General seated

Sketch by S. Hall—Public Archives of Canada

On August 27, 1881, S. Hall made a sketch of the Hudson's Bay Post mill at Prince Albert and the archway decorated for the visit of the Marquis of Lorne.

on Chief Factor Clarke's veranda, with the Indians gathered on the lawn in front. The Marquis, dressed in a frock coat, wore the star of some chivalric order on his shoulder. Among the Indians, White Cap, a Sioux, was attired in the handsomest costume; like the Marquis, he wore a badge of native honor, for from his shoulder dangled some twenty pale-face scalps, souvenirs of the Minnesota Massacre.

. At 4:30 P.M. on August 26 the Marquis of Lorne and his suite embarked on the **Northcote,** and the following morning arrived in Prince Albert. At the steamboat landing an arch had been erected in His Excellency's honor. According to a journalistic report, it had been decorated with the trophies of the chase and the rewards of husbandry, and carried a welcoming inscription in English, Gaelic, and Cree. Unfortunately for the plans of the reception committee, the weather was unco-operative and rain poured down. The reception was held in the· saloon of the **Northcote,** into which more than two hundred people pressed.

The only vice-regal reception ever held aboard a Saskatchewan steamer was described as follows:

The reception committee, two and two abreast, followed by the whole of the people assembled, gathered in the saloon of the steamer, until every inch of space was filled, when His Lordship the Bishop of Saskatchewan stepped forward, and in a most impressive manner read the address of welcome of the people of the settlement, His excellency . . . then read his reply of acknowledgement than which nothing could have been more appropriate and pleasing to the hearts of the listeners. After the presentation had been made, when every person on the boat had had his hand shaken by His Excellency, then such shouts arose that had never yet been heard in Prince Albert, and raised serious doubts as to whether the steamer's roof could stand a repetition of such hearty shouts of welcome.[2]

The Marquis of Lorne and his party boarded the **Lily** at 2:30 P.M. for the trip up-river to Battleford, where they disembarked on August 30.

The Marquis left a vivid description of a Saskatchewan river steamer in his book "Canadian Pictures, drawn with pen and pencil."

The first thing which seems odd to a European is that there is only one paddle wheel, and this

Sketch by S. Hall—Public Archives of Canada

The LILY, *August 30, 1881, with members of the Marquis of Lorne's suite in foreground.*

single wheel is placed at the stern, so that the craft looks like an upturned wheelbarrow. The feature which will, secondly, seem the oddest is a curious erection of beams on the forward deck. Two things, like the gyns used in lifting heavy weights, are placed on each side. The heavy weight to be lifted in this case is the vessel itself. As soon as very shallow water is struck, two long beams are put over the side, the wheel astern churns up the water, and the ship is fairly lifted on these, as a lame man is on crutches, for a few feet over the obstacle. The poles are then hoisted, and put forward again into the sand, and another step onward is made. Where such a rig is not provided, the only means of making progress consists in getting out a hawser and attaching it to something on the bank. The capstan is then manned and the hawser hauled upon, and with much shouting, rocking of the boat, and convulsive effort of the engines, step by step, way is gained, until deeper water is reached.

Meanwhile, the **Northcote** steamed on down the river. There was great disappointment at Cumberland House and The Pas that the Governor General and his party were not aboard. At Cumberland, when the **Northcote** hove in sight, the fort fired a salute of seventeen guns, and the whole populace of a hundred people, led by the portly figure of Chief Factor Horace Belanger, waited on the dock. Belanger had an address in English and French ready to present.[3]

Cumberland House was the oldest inland station of the Hudson's Bay Company, having been established in 1774 by Samuel Hearne. The post stood on the south shore of Cumberland Lake (earlier called Pine Island Lake). The lake was separated from the Saskatchewan River, which ran parallel to it, by about two miles of low-lying land. The lake drained into the Saskatchewan by two short rivers, the Bigstone and the Tearing. Inside the stockaded fort were a number of log buildings, the largest of which was a great warehouse with its machinery for pressing furs and for making pemmican. In 1873 the post collected and sent out 240,000 muskrat skins. A brass sundial stood in the enclosure of the fort, a memento of the visit three decades earlier of the Arctic explorer, Sir John Franklin. About ten acres of land was in cultivation around the fort, and there were a few scattered homes of Indians, and the Catholic and Anglican chapels.

Tuttle, C. R.: Our north land

Cumberland House. An engraving from a photograph taken in 1884 by John A. Cadenhead of the Otto Klotz party.

The season of 1881 had been a successful one for the Saskatchewan steamers. At its conclusion the **Lily** and the **Northcote** were drawn out for the winter at Cumberland House with the intention of sailing them earlier in the season than was possible if they went into winter berth at Grand Rapids. (Cedar Lake did not clear of ice as soon as the river above.) The cargoes for the first upbound voyages in 1882 had already been brought to Cumberland House. The **Saskatchewan Herald,** in its final shipping news for the season, reported:

Shippers will be glad to learn that not a single piece of private freight remains at Grand Rapids.[4]

Chapter 12

WINNIPEG STEAMBOAT COMPANY
ON THE SASKATCHEWAN

A LONG THE SASKATCHEWAN in 1881 there were rumors of new companies and additional steamboats coming to the river, but these rumors were not to reach fruition until the navigation season of 1882. The **Herald,** at Battleford, reported that the charter of the Saskatchewan Transportation and Trading Company[1] had been acquired by an English syndicate with the intention to put a line of steamers on the river. Late in the autumn the **Bulletin,** of Edmonton, reported, nearer the truth, that the Winnipeg and Western Transportation Company would take over steamboat transportation on the river from the Hudson's Bay Company. Another company with Winnipeg headquarters, the North West Navigation Company, was also involved in the transfer of riverboats to the Saskatchewan.

The most obvious reason for the interest in the transport business was the steady expansion of settlement and increasing commerce along the North Saskatchewan and the lower part of the south branch. The two steamers operated by the Hudson's Bay Com-

Manitoba Archives

The Winnipeg & Western Transportation Company's steamboat CITY OF WINNIPEG photographed in 1881.

75

pany were not adequate to carry the traffic after they were thrown open as carriers to the general public. The Company had been ready in 1880 to build and place at least one more sternwheeler on the river in time for the 1881 season, providing the Dominion Government undertook the removal of obstacles and hazards to navigation, but the procrastination of the Department of Public Works ruined this plan.

The decision to run the Canadian Pacific Railway line two hundred miles to the south, instead of along the valley of the North Saskatchewan as proposed in earlier surveys, changed the prospects of steamboats on the river. Some years of profitable operation could be expected before rail lines reached the Saskatchewan valley.

In 1881 the two Winnipeg steamboat companies knew that the prosperous river traffic on the Red and Assiniboine rivers would shortly end. The first locomotive reached Winnipeg aboard the **Dakota** on October 8, 1877. Decorated with flags and banners, the boat docked to the blowing of mill whistles and the ringing of church bells. On board, Miss Racine, the colored stewardess, clanged the ship's bell steadily amid the pandemonium; she was unwittingly ringing the knell for steamboating on the Red River. The railway connecting Winnipeg with St. Paul was completed in the spring of 1879. In 1881 the Canadian Pacific track-laying crews were building along the Assiniboine toward Brandon. The two boat companies, unless they wanted to beach their boats, had no choice but to transfer them to the Saskatchewan River.

The Winnipeg and Western Transportation Com-

pany had been formed in 1878, with a capitalization
of $50,000.² The objective of the Company was to

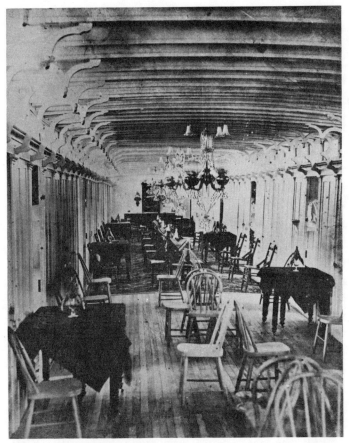

Manitoba Archives

*In 1881 Winnipeg photographer I. Bennetto took this photograph of
the interior of the steamboat* CITY OF WINNIPEG *capturing the
relative luxury of the fittings. To a greater or lesser extent other
steamboats would be fitted in a similar manner. Note the paneling,
the chandeliers and the wall-to-wall carpeting covering a section of
the deck.*

operate a freighting business by steamboat on the waterways of Manitoba, the District of Keewatin, and in the Northwest Territories.

That season the new Company operated two boats, the **Alpha** and the **Cheyenne.**[3] By the spring of 1881, the Company had acquired from the Red River Transportation Company (Kittson's line) at least two further steamers, the **Minnesota** and the **Manitoba,** and had had them lengthened by nearly fifty feet in a shipyard at Grand Forks, Dakota. This major addition may have weakened the two sternwheelers and have been a factor in the destruction of the first by the rough waters of Lake Winnipeg, of the other by spring ice at Sturgeon River. In the spring of 1881, and upon the change to British registry, the **Minnesota** was renamed the **City of Winnipeg.**

The North West Navigation Company was formed in 1881.[4] Its charter permitted this Company to run steamers on the Red, Assiniboine, and Saskatchewan rivers, and on lakes Winnipeg, Manitoba, and Winnipegosis. The Company's charter also permitted the operation of tramways. The North West Navigation Company and the Winnipeg and Western Transportation Company were apparently consolidated through an interlocking directorship a few months after the formation of the former, with Peter McArthur as general manager.

Of the men who organized the North West Navigation Company, three must be singled out for attention. William Robinson, of Selkirk, was a captain who would own and sail vessels on Lake Winnipeg for many years, mostly in connection with the lumber

Peter McArthur, early Winnipeg shipbuilder, and the man who directed the warping of three steamboats up Grand Rapids at the mouth of the Saskatchewan River.

C. J. Brydges, Land Commissioner of the Hudson's Bay Company, and a man who urged the Government to make improvements to the Saskatchewan waterway.

and fish trades. Peter McArthur was a Winnipeg lumberman interested in building sternwheel steamers; McArthur commissioned the building of the **North West** and the **Marquis.** The third, C. J. Brydges, was Land Commissioner of the Hudson's Bay Company; his name on the roster suggests the connection of the steamboat company with the fur company.

The close co-operation of the two existing steamboat companies may have been influenced in part by the threat of competition from still another company. The Saskatchewan Transportation and Trading Company was incorporated on July 10, 1882,[5] and was capitalized at $50,000. The charter provided for the construction, acquiring, and chartering of new steamboats and barges on lakes Winnipeg, Manitoba, etc.

What was the relationship of the former carrier on the Saskatchewan to the two Winnipeg steamboat companies? The Hudson's Bay Company references are to an agreement with only the Winnipeg and Western Transportation Company, in which it had a controlling interest.[6] The interlocking of directorships with the North West Navigation Company probably came later.

The shareholders of the Hudson's Bay Company were informed at a meeting on June 27, 1882, that the Company had gone out of direct involvement in the steamboat traffic:

> The Governor and Committee have sanctioned an arrangement recommended to them by the Commissioners, of the company, under which the 'Northcote', 'Lily', and 'Colvile' have been made over to the local steamboat company, formed for the purpose of carrying freight and passengers on Lake Winnipeg and the rivers in the Manitoba and the North-West Territory. The terms under which the steamers have been transferred include the retention, on behalf of the Company, of an interest in the Steamboat Company in proportion to the valuation of their own Steamers and on arrangement for the carriage of the Company's goods and supplies in accordance with the requirements of the trade.

The Shipping Register of the Port of Winnipeg recorded the date of sale of the steam vessels, and adds confusion to the relationship between the steamboat companies. The **Northcote** and the **Lily** are shown as being sold by the H.B. Co. to the W. & W. T. Co.

Manitoba Archives

This photo, taken about 1884, shows the MARQUIS tied up alongside a storage shed on the Saskatchewan River.

on July 18, 1883, a year later than the arrangement; there is always the possibility that the year was a slip of a clerk's pen. The **Manitoba** always belonged to the W. & W. T. Co. The **North West** was sold by Peter McArthur to N. W. N. Co. on March 15, 1882, and resold to the W. & W. T. Co. on April 16, 1884. The **Marquis,** according to the Shipping Register, always belonged to the W. & W. T. Co. The lake steamer **Colvile** was sold by the H.B. Co. to the W. & W. T. Co. on June 24, 1882, and resold to the N.W.N. Co. on February 8, 1884. The lake steamer **Princess** always belonged to the N.W.N. Co. Thus, by the navigation season of 1884, the five sternwheelers on the Saskatchewan were owned by the W. & W.T. Co., in which the Hudson's Bay Company had a controlling interest, while the two lake steamers were in the possession of the N.W.N. Co., which seems to have contracted with the fur company to supply its posts around Lake Winnipeg, and with the W. & W.T. Co. to transport its cargoes to and from Grand Rapids.

Peter McArthur, in his reminiscences many years later, said that Captain Robinson was first charged with the responsibility of getting the Red River stern-wheelers across stormy Lake Winnipeg and up Grand Rapids. When Robinson lost the **City of Winnipeg,** McArthur was assigned the task of conveying the steamers across. He succeeded in getting three river steamers to the Saskatchewan and warped up the rapids in 1882.

McArthur claimed, in his reminiscences, that he was discharged as general manager of the Winnipeg and Western Transportation Company because of liquor. In the Northwest Territories a strict prohibition was in force. The steamboat company wanted liquor carried to Edmonton in the hold of a vessel. McArthur refused to countenance smuggling and was summarily dismissed.

Chapter 13

TRANSFER OF VESSELS
TO THE SASKATCHEWAN

THE FIRST BOAT to be transferred from the
Red River to the Saskatchewan River was the
S. S. City of Winnipeg. Formerly the S. S.
Minnesota, she had been enlarged at Grand Forks,
Minnesota, in the winter of 1880-81, and changed
from American to British registry in the spring of
1881.

The following is a journalistic account of the enlarged steamer upon her arrival in Winnipeg on
April 29:

The Minnesota presents quite an imposing appearance, as the result of her enlarged dimensions and numerous improvements. Seventy feet
of her hull, cabin and deck have been constructed
entirely new, thus making the steamer forty feet
longer than before. The total length of the hull
is now 170 feet, thus making the vessel altogether,
including the wheel, 190 feet long. The addition
gives a fine new forecastle and also ten more
staterooms than before. The increased comfort of
the passengers has been provided for by placing

spring mattresses in all the staterooms. A large and convenient wash room and barber shop has been added, the water for which is supplied from a reservoir on the hurricane deck. The reservoir is filled by means of a force pump below, and there are pipes to carry away overboard the water which has been used. In the middle of the boat are gangways leading out upon the guards—a convenience which did not before exist. The guards are some two feet wider than before. Passengers will now find it very convenient to take a constitutional before breakfast. Some of the most important of all the improvements are noticeable in the steerage. A strong railing four and a half feet high is placed along the outer edges on both sides from fore to aft, thus affording security against the drowning accidents which have been so numerous in former years on vessels navigating our northwestern rivers. Steerage passengers will be made more comfortable than heretofore by means of berths, which are to be provided. Especial facilities are offered for the shipping of stock. One hundred horses can be taken without difficulty. The hold will be eighteen inches deeper in the forward part than before, making it 5½ feet deep. The vessel will draw eight inches less of water than before. The new smoke stacks are lofty and handsome. Derricks and spars, with guys and pulleys have been provided, which will greatly facilitate the process of landing.[1]

Three weeks later the same newspaper reported that the sternwheeler was being fitted out with new carpets, mammoth pier glasses, and a piano.

Throughout the summer the **City of Winnipeg** plied the Assiniboine River. In mid-August she was disabled and had to be towed down to Winnipeg for repairs. At this time the Winnipeg and Western Transportation Company made the decision that she, instead of the **Manitoba,** would be the first vessel transferred to the Saskatchewan River. The estimated cost of putting her into commission there was $5,000.

On September 6 the **City of Winnipeg** left Selkirk for the perilous trip—for a riverboat—across Lake Winnipeg, in tow by the **Princess,** Captain William Robinson in command. The **Princess** was a new lake steamer on her maiden voyage. She was a sidewheeler of 289 tons with a length of 132 feet, and boasting twenty-six passenger cabins. She was later converted to a screw steamer. Many years later this lake steamer was to break up in a similar autumn storm to the one which buffeted her on her maiden voyage. (She was lost on August 9, 1906, off Swampy Island, when her boilers plummeted through her bottom; six crew members were carried to their death.)

The **City of Winnipeg** was in charge of James Sheets,[2] who would spend several seasons on the Saskatchewan. He had been a riverman in the American West from 1844 before coming to the Red River in 1876 as mate of the **Manitoba.** He also sailed on the Assiniboine River for one or two seasons. He was to be captain of the **North West** for eight seasons on the Saskatchewan, latterly as superintendent of operations for the Winnipeg and Western Transportation Company. Captain Jimmy Sheets was a popular skipper with crews and passengers, and was said to have had a fine baritone voice for leading the singing in a vessel's saloon in the evenings.

The **City of Winnipeg's** machinery had been partly removed and taken aboard the **Princess,** but she carried in her hold a cargo of 42,000 board feet of lumber.

Shortly after getting out on the lake, the vessels encountered the first of the equinoctial storms and had to seek shelter in a harbor near Dog's Head. Later, another storm came up, and an anchorage was found at Swampy Island. The voyage then continued successfully until off Long Point, about sixty miles from the mouth of the Saskatchewan. A third storm came up, blowing a strong beam wind which started **battering** the fragile riverboat to pieces. The **Princess** struggled for two days with her tow, but finally the order was given to cut the line of the doomed vessel, which then drifted before the wind for five miles. Hitting a rockbound shore, one side of the **City** was torn off and her deck burst loose.

A newspaper account describes the night of the wreck through the captain's eyes:

Captain Sheets says the night of the wreck was a terrible one. The sea ran mountain high, and the City, although of fragile build, stood the storm bravely for a while. She then tossed and pitched and rolled, her chains snapped, her timbers creaked and strained, and it was not until the cabin was taken off and danger was apprehended for her consort, the Princess, that she was cut loose and left to drift ashore . . . Captain Sheets was the last to leave the craft of which he had proven himself so excellent and popular a commander.[3]

After the vessel broke upon the beach, Captain Sheets salvaged the lumber and some of the ship's material. The salvagers, eight men in all, set off for Grand Rapids, but still another storm came up on the lake. They had to put in at Little Horse Island, where their boat was damaged. To repair it, they extracted the cotton batting from their bed rolls for caulking, and burned the seat of the boat for the nails they needed. The men were on short rations before they finally reached the safety of Grand Rapids.

The loss of the **City of Winnipeg** was estimated at $20,000.

The following summer, 1882, three additional sternwheelers reached the Saskatchewan River. These were the **North West**, the **Manitoba**, and the **Marquis**.

The first of these to be successfully sailed across Lake Winnipeg to Grand Rapids was the **North West**. Her hold was filled with coal-oil barrels to keep her afloat should her low gunnels ship water. She crossed the lake under her own steam but was escorted by the lake steamer **Princess**. The **North West** arrived at the lower end of Grand Rapids on July 4. She started the ascent on a Wednesday in July. A line half a mile in length was laid out. On the first day the ship was warped up two lengths of the line. What excitement! — the taut line and the creaking capstan; the racing engines of the steamer and the thrashing paddle wheel at her stern; and above all, the roar of the frothing waters.

On Thursday, the capstan broke under the strain.

88

S. C. Ells Collection—Public Archives of Canada

Winnipeg waterfront, June, 1882. The NORTH WEST *is in the foreground of the picture, the* MANITOBA *is docked astern. The man wearing a long coat on the hurricane deck is Captain Jerry Webber.*

On Friday, the steamer's paddle wheel was damaged. On Saturday, the capstan again gave out. On Sunday, the **Northcote** dropped down-river as close as she dared to the rapids, and anchored herself by snubbing a line to the bank. She gave the struggling **North West** a pull and brought her half way over the brink of the last rapid. At the crucial moment the **Northcote's** capstan broke, leaving the **North West** balanced on the edge of the last pitch. Under the terrific strain a hog chain broke, and the ship was in danger of being broken in two. Fortunately, the main chains held. The **North West** was pulled to safety.[4]

The **North West** had been built the previous year, 1881, at Moorhead, Minnesota, for Peter McArthur of Winnipeg. Her builder was Captain John

The NORTH WEST *at Battleford, 1885.*

S. Irish. In the registry of the Dominion Department of Marine she is described as a vessel 200 feet long, 33 feet in the beam, with a 4.5-foot depth. Her registered tonnage was 305, her gross 425. She was powered by double-level engines with cylinders 16 inches in diameter and a 5-foot stroke, which received power from two solid steel boilers of 10 flues each. The cabin was 120 feet long by 22 feet wide, with berths for eighty passengers; two of these were elegantly fitted up as bridal suites. The cabin boasted a piano, the first steamer on the Red River to have one. The second deck was ten feet clear of the first, and the hurricane deck stood eight feet above the second, and had a pilot house mounted on top. The **North West** was to prove herself to be the most successful of the Saskatchewan River steamers, mostly because her draft of eighteen inches was slightly less than that of the other steamers. The sternwheeler cost over $27,000.[5]

The last two river steamers, the **Marquis** and the **Manitoba**, arrived at Grand Rapids on July 25. The

Manitoba Archives

Shown are the bow of the MARQUIS and the stern of the NORTH WEST. The photograph would be taken prior to the opening of navigation since the paddles, removed to prevent damage by ice, have not been bolted to the wheel. The word "Winnipeg" refers to the home office of the shipping company where the boat was registered. The photo was probably taken at Cumberland House in the spring of 1884.

Manitoba came across under steam, the **Marquis** towed by the **Princess.** The **Marquis** was in an incompleted state, for scarcely any of her machinery had yet been installed.

The hull of the **Marquis** had been laid down that spring in Winnipeg at the foot of Bannantyne Street. She was built for Peter McArthur by a Mr. Gregory, a shipbuilder from La Crosse, Wisconsin. The largest of the sternwheel steamers ever to ply the waters of the Canadian Prairies, she was 201 feet in length, 33.5 feet wide, and 5.3 feet in depth. Her hull was of white oak, brought from Wisconsin. Her engine-room was 55 feet long, and equipped with two horizontal, high-pressure engines of 83.74 horsepower. The engines were manufactured by the Iowa Iron Works of Dubuque, Iowa. She had three boilers, and was capable of generating 125 pounds of steam to the square inch. Her cylinder bore was 19 inches, and her piston stroke was 6 feet. She had four balanced rudders hung from the stern ahead of the paddle wheel. Her registered tonnage was 474.87, while her gross tonnage was 753.76. Her draft was 25 inches, and her speed was up to 16 miles per hour. In the Shipping Registry a penciled note gives her cost as $55,000,[6] but another estimate valued her at $61,000. She had been named after the Governor General of the day, the Marquis of Lorne.

The only machinery in the **Marquis** when she started up Grand Rapids was that connected with her "niggers." She went ahead, pulling herself the length of a line, and then assisted the **Manitoba.** When the two steamers had pulled themselves a third

Manitoba Hydro

Strip of limestone bank on south side of river, Grand Rapids. It was rocks like these that cut the main line of the MARQUIS.

of the way up the rapids, the smaller **Manitoba** was left tied to the bank while the **Marquis** proceeded alone so that the **Northcote** could assist her before departing for up-river. At the last pitch the **Northcote** came down as far as she dared, and after snubbing to the bank, attached a line to the **Marquis.** The **Marquis** laid two lines to the shore, and when the three "niggers" got to work she was easily pulled to safety. Once, during her ten days of struggle, she scraped a precipitous bank, causing a large mass of rock to cascade down upon her deck. One night the main line by which she was snubbed, chaffed on a sharp rock until the line gave way, but fortunately, a smaller line held until the main cable could be repaired. She reached the higher level on August 4.

The machinery for the **Marquis** was brought across Lake Winnipeg by the **Princess** on her next trip. Engineers and carpenters were also brought out to complete her. This largest and most luxurious of the Saskatchewan steamers was not in service until September 25.

The third vessel to be warped up Grand Rapids, the **Manitoba,** was captained that first season by Aaron Raymond Russell.[7] Born in Franklin, Pennsylvania, in 1829, he had taken at an early age to steamboating on the Ohio and other inland rivers. From 1871 he was a mate and captain on the Red River, and during the 1880 and 1881 navigation seasons, on the Assiniboine River.

The **Manitoba** was almost as old a boat as the **Northcote,** for she had been built in 1875 at Fargo, Dakota Territory, for service on the Red River. In

94

Glenbow Foundation

The MANITOBA about 1880 before she was lengthened by fifty feet, and while still under American registry as indicated by the flag.

her first season, she was rammed by the **International** and sunk, but was raised and put back into service the same summer. In the winter of 1880-81 at Grand Forks, Minnesota, the **Manitoba** was lengthened by fifty feet to make her 190 feet in length. Her gross tonnage was 405.94.

The **Manitoba** was a ship with a jinx. In her first three years of service, 1875 to 1878, she had no fewer than three collisions, had a minor fire in her hold, and lost a passenger overboard.[8] She would be crushed by ice on the Saskatchewan in the spring of 1885.

Chapter 14

NAVIGATION SEASON 1882

THE WINNIPEG and Western Transportation Company moved 1,468 tons[1] of freight from Grand Rapids up the Saskatchewan by steamer in 1882. In addition, early in the season, prior to being transferred to the transport company, the **Northcote** moved all the freight in storage at Cumberland House, perhaps more than a hundred tons. Under the new management, the **Northcote** carried 612 tons. Of the new steamboats, the **North West** made the best showing as a carrier, moving 558 tons in three voyages. The **Manitoba** and the **Marquis,** sailing late from Grand Rapids, took only one cargo apiece part way up the river. The **Lily** was not in service that season.

At the beginning of the season the **Northcote,** with Captain Webber again in command, made an early start, leaving Cumberland House on May 8. She discharged freight en route, arriving at Edmonton on May 28 with fifty tons of freight for the Hudson's Bay Company, and a small quantity for private individuals. Included were 700 sacks of flour from the Prince Albert settlement for the Peace River trade, wheat from Battleford, and 123 pieces of goods for the Athabasca country. On the return she took on board 14,528 pounds of furs. The water was in good stage, and the ship reached Grand Rapids on June 5.

The **Northcote** on her first through trip from Grand Rapids broke all previous records. She left on June 18 with a cargo and seventy-five passengers, and reached Edmonton in fourteen days. She had ascended Cole's Falls, which sometimes took four days, in a day and a half. At Edmonton she debarked 103,415 pounds of freight for the Hudson's Bay Company, and a smaller quantity for other consignees. Her return cargo consisted of 6,680 pounds of fur and 167 pounds of castoreum for the Company, and in addition, shingles for Victoria, and shingles and lumber for Battleford.

The **Northcote** made at least one more trip to Edmonton during the season, and other trips to some of the lower river ports.

The **North West,** after being successfully warped up Grand Rapids, lost no time in loading cargo from the warehouse above the Rapids. She was under the command of Captain Sheets. Her log from Grand Rapids to Battleford may be regarded as fairly typical for up-river voyages:

July 12—Left Grand Rapids for Edmonton at 9:40 a.m. with 180 tons of freight. As we steamed up the river we passed the Northcote and were greeted with three rousing cheers from her crew and the inhabitants of the post, who all turned out to see us off. Arrived at the foot of Roche Rouge Rapids at 10:45. Finished laying our first

Saloon of the MARQUIS some years after she was abandoned. The picture gives an indication of her length. Note cabin doors.

line and started up the rapids at 11:50. Laid our second line at 4:40 and were over the rapids by 6:15 p.m. Entered Cross Lake at seven o'clock and reached the foot of the Demi-Charge at 7:35, where we tied up for the night.

July 13—Started at 5:30, laid a line and were over the rapids by eight o'clock. Entered the Narrows and stopped at a woodpile at 10:15, where we were detained until four o'clock by the high wind. Stopped at Grigg's Harbor, 6:20, and after taking on spars we left to cross Cedar Lake at 6:55 p.m. Were abreast of Rabbit Point at 7:15 and passed at 9:10. Laid up for the night at the Che-ma-wa-win at ten.

July 14—Started at 3 a.m. and proceeded until 9:45 when we stopped to repair the wheel. Started again at 5 p.m., and arrived at The Pas at 10:45 where we took on wood and left at midnight.

July 15—Running all last night. Reached Two Portages at 8:50 a.m., and after wooding up we once more got underway at ten o'clock. Entered Big Stone River at 12:55, and landed at Cumberland at 2 p.m. Left at three o'clock. While laid up at a woodpile we had to repair our wheel and did not get started up the river until 6:15. Laid up for the night at 10:30.

July 16—Started at 2 a.m. and got over Tobin's Rapids without lining at noon. Tied up for the night at eleven.

July 17—Started at two o'clock and reached Fort à la Corne at 7:30 p.m.

July 18—Left at 6:30 a.m. and arrived at the

Forks at 7:45 p.m. Entered the North Branch and tied up at the foot of Cole's Falls at 8:15. Two more wheel-arms broken, and we have to send to Prince Albert for wheel-arms and a carpenter.
July 19—Started at 2:30 a.m. and were over the falls at 8:15 p.m.
July 20—Arrived at Prince Albert at 7:45 a.m. and left at 7:15 p.m.
July 21—Arrived at Carlton at 8 a.m. and left at nine.
July 22—In evening arrived at Battleford.[2]

The arrival of the new steamer created a flurry of excitement at each of the river ports. The following describes her arrival at Battleford:

On the evening of the 22nd ult. word was passed about the streets that a steamboat was coming up the Saskatchewan and as it had been rumored for some time that a new boat would shortly ply on the river, it was not many minutes before a large crowd had congregated at the landing to ascertain whether it was the Northcote or the new one. The moment the whistle sounded, however, all doubts were dispelled as it was a strange voice that awakened the echoes of the valley of the Saskatchewan. When she approached the landing, she was boarded by the curious.

The **North West** reached Edmonton five days later. En route from Grand Rapids she had lost a total of seventy-two hours through breakages of the paddle wheel; otherwise she would have broken the record the **Northcote** had established the previous month. She had carried 182 tons of freight to Prince

Albert, 215 tons between that point and Battleford, and 132 tons to Edmonton.

The **North West** set sail from Grand Rapids on her second voyage with 206 tons of cargo and ten passengers on August 11. As she cast off from the wharf it appeared for a few tense minutes as though she might go down the Grand Rapids. The incident is described in the diary of a Church of England missionary, the Reverend Abraham Cowley:

> August 11, 1882. Started about 3:35 a.m. The North West got foul of the Marquis a new vessel which is being prepared for river navigation & caused some delay. I was really frightened when I saw the paddle wheel of our boat against the bow of the Marquis & the head of the North West swinging round in the current toward Grand Rapids. But thank God the Capt. kept cool & self-possessed, ordering the anchor to be ready & as soon as the wheel was free, plied the steamer in great force, brought the vessel round & stemmed the current right nobly. The danger of an involuntary descent down the Grand Rapids, with the almost certain prospect of the utter destruction of the steamboat & great loss of life was thus by God's mercy averted & we were thankful.[3]

The **North West** later made a third voyage.

As for the **Manitoba,** she was late in getting up Grand Rapids and into commission. According to a Winnipeg report her paddle wheel had been badly smashed in the ascent, and this no doubt caused the delay in sailing. She passed The Pas upward bound on

Public Archives of Canada

The MARQUIS poling over a shallow.

September 1. On arrival at Cole's Falls, she found the water too low for her to ascend. The freight for Prince Albert was landed on the riverbank and left, much to the annoyance of the shippers who were put to the trouble and expense of hiring carts to transport the goods to the settlement. The remainder of the cargo was stored at Fort à la Corne.

The **Marquis** was not fitted with all her machinery until very late in the season. The luxury liner of the river sailed from Grand Rapids on September 25 with 131 tons, and reached Cumberland on October 9. She arrived back at her home port on October 21. The length of time taken on the voyage suggests that the passage was laborious.

Chapter 15

THE CUT-OFF

H OW IRONIC that the very season that a fleet of steamboats began operating on the Saskatchewan the navigation channel should be severed, with the river's flow spilling into the swamps and off-shoots of Cumberland Lake. The Saskatchewan River originally ran south of and parallel to Cumberland Lake; the lake drained into the river through two short streams. Some seventy miles west of Cumberland House the Saskatchewan flowed through flat, marshy ground where it was easy for the river to cut new channels. As early as 1865, some of the waters of the river entered the Sturgeon River, which connected with Cumberland Lake, but beginning in 1882, an increasing quantity of it flowed in this direction, entering the lake by several channels. By the autumn of 1883, the old bed of the Saskatchewan for more than fifty miles would be dry; in the spring of 1884, all the ice from the upper river entered the lake.[1] The dissipation of the river's flow into new channels and rivulets made navigation of this section of the river difficult, and sometimes impossible, for the steamboats.

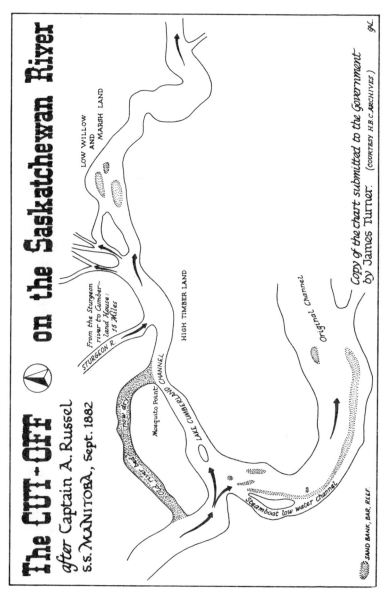

The CUT-OFF on the Saskatchewan River

after Captain A. Russel
S.S. MANITOBA, Sept. 1882

LOW WILLOW
AND
MARSH LAND

From the Sturgeon
river to Cumber-
land House: 15 Miles

STURGEON R.

HIGH TIMBER LAND

Mosquito Point

now dry

now dry

LAKE CUMBERLAND CHANNEL

Original Channel

Steamboat low water channel

SAND BANK, BAR, REEF.

Copy of the chart submitted to the Government
by James Turner. (COURTESY H.B.C. ARCHIVES)

106

The break-through from the Saskatchewan to the Sturgeon was at the tip of a long sharp bend to the northward, known to the rivermen as Mosquito Point. About 1875, an ice jam at the tip of the point had caused the river to cut a channel across the base, which was henceforth known as The Cut-Off since it saved several miles.[2] Perhaps it was ice action again which turned the river's course in 1882 up the east side of Mosquito Point and across-country to the Sturgeon River and its swamps. Of the several channels through the swamp of bulrushes by which the Saskatchewan's water finally entered Cumberland Lake, the best known were the Lake Channel, the Steamboat Channel, and the Angling Channel; the latter became the canoe route.

On the first voyage of the 1882 season, the **Northcote** experienced difficulty in the original river channel because of low water and shoals. Chief Factor Belanger of Cumberland House was asked to have men explore and mark distinctly with buoys the main channel through the marsh.[3]

Mr. James Turner, a traveler aboard the **North West** on her last downward voyage of the 1882 season, wrote to the Dominion Department of Public Works on the situation below The Cut-Off:

As regards the navigation from the Cut-Off, I am afraid, if not altogether, at any rate, for a portion of each season, the original channel to Big Stone River, say 73 miles, must be abandoned, and the new channel via Cumberland Lake adopted, which will be unfortunate, seeing this channel is not to be depended on and light draught steamers are wholly unsuited and very dangerous for such lake navigation—the feasibility, at a reasonable cost, of closing up the Cumberland Lake channel, and throwing the whole stream into the original channel, must however be decided by engineering ability, as the river has already cut out the new channel to such an extent as may make the change a matter of serious expense and difficulty even although all the necessary timber —willows and stone for the purpose are to be had of suitable size and quality in abundance on the spot.[4]

The **Northcote** followed the original river channel, but experienced great difficulty getting through because of the lack of water. Captain Russell, on the **Manitoba,** followed the original channel for a mile and a half, but finding only eighteen inches of water, sailed back to The Cut-Off. Exploring the Sturgeon River route, he found the channel intricate but containing as much as eight feet of water.

Captain Russell had a genuine interest in the solution of navigational problems, for he had spent a season, the summer of 1869, in command of the **C. F. Caffrey,** a sidewheel snag boat engaged in "scraping" the sand off the high places in the steamboat channel on the upper Mississippi from Lacrosse to St. Paul. We are indebted to him for a map of The Cut-Off area on the Saskatchewan.

The danger of being trapped in the ill-defined channels through the swamp between Cumberland Lake and The Cut-Off caused the river captains to tie up for the season earlier than they might otherwise have done.[5] Consequently, at least 500 tons of freight had to be left at Cumberland House for the winter.

The storage facilities of this ancient fur depot were taxed by the quantity of cargo awaiting shipment up-river. Of the five boat cargoes, two were consigned to the Hudson's Bay Company, the other three to other business concerns and private individuals.[6] The warehouse at Cumberland House, 80 by 25 feet, was stacked ten feet high with freight, while non-perishable goods were piled outside.

More goods lay at Grand Rapids, but most shippers had the **Princess** bring their freight back to Winnipeg. The last group of Saskatchewan-bound passengers to sail out to Grand Rapids that season had to return because the riverboats had been beached.

The failure of the Winnipeg and Western Transportation Company to move all the freight to its destination caused inconvenience and hardship to many people in the Saskatchewan country. At Prince Albert, in October, the Hudson's Bay Company store was reported not to have a single chest of tea in stock. The Dominion Inspector of Surveys, W. F. King, had shipped between ten and twelve tons of supplies and equipment from Winnipeg in the spring of 1882, consigned to survey parties dividing the land into townships along the upper Saskatchewan. Some of the survey crews went short of rations during the winter when the supplies failed to get up-river. Indeed, delivery was not made until two years later, for Mr. King, reporting on the land surveys for the summer of 1884, wrote as follows:

. . . Some 10 or 12 tons of provisions, which had

been forwarded from Winnipeg in 1882 by the Saskatchewan River steamers, and which were still lying at Victoria, were brought from that place to Edmonton.[7]

The confidence of shippers in the reliability of the Saskatchewan steamboats to deliver freight was destroyed.

Chapter 16

RIVER IMPROVEMENTS

THE HUDSON'S BAY COMPANY, as operator of the two Saskatchewan steamers, had begun pressing upon the Dominion Government in the summer of 1879 the necessity of improving the navigability of the river by the removal of certain obstacles. Parliament, in the session of 1880-81, voted $20,000 for the improvement of the Saskatchewan, but work did not commence until the summer of 1883. Thereafter, surveys or improvements were undertaken each summer until 1888 or 1889, but the major improvements were executed in the seasons of 1883 and 1884, under the direction of E. A. Burbank.

The arguments for improving the steamboat channel were four in number. First, there was the obvious advantage of reducing the risk to the steamboats of damage from boulders. The second was to reduce the delays in warping up rapids so that the time taken for each voyage could be shortened, and more trips made by each steamer in a season. Thirdly, if the channel were deeper at the difficult spots, then the boats could carry heavier cargoes. Finally, a deepened channel would enable boats to find sufficient water in the late summer and autumn when the river was normally in low stage; this, it was predicted, would extend the navigation season by four to six weeks.

Mr. Brydges, Land Commissioner of the Hudson's Bay Company, wrote to the Minister of Public Works on June 21, 1879, urging the early beginning of work on the Saskatchewan River.[1] This first letter specified those rapids and channels where improvements were required. In reply, the Department said that nothing could be undertaken immediately since that year's estimates contained no money for this work. The following autumn the Department proposed that the obstacles listed be removed at public expense, but that the Hudson's Bay Company build the piers needed to assist the boats in warping up the Roche Rouge[2] and Demi-Charge rapids. On behalf of the Company, Brydges agreed to this proposal.[3]

In November, 1880, the Department of Public Works obtained authorization to spend $2,000 on the dredging of a channel through the bar at the mouth of the Red River, and to prepare and submit estimates to the next session of Parliament on the cost of the work required to improve the Saskatchewan.

The Department of Public Works detailed an engineer to make a report on the Saskatchewan in the summer of 1881, but he was occupied during the whole of the season in examining Lake Manitoba. Writing to the Minister, Sir Hector Langevin, on January 10, 1882, Mr. Brydges expressed disappointment that no improvements had been begun on the Saskatchewan:

112

You never did anything about the improvements on the Saskatchewan River, for which a sum was put in last year's Estimates.

Additional steamers are being built this winter for the river, and there is every prospect of a large traffic between Edmonton and the forks of the Saskatchewan.

I was very disappointed that nothing was done last year. I felt sure that you would have carried out your promised programme.

On February 21 Brydges again corresponded with the Minister, saying that it had been suggested that officers of the Company, in vicinities where river improvements were needed, might be in charge of the work. While the Company had no desire to incur the labor and responsibility of the undertaking, on request it would do so.

In response to this proposal an order in council was passed on March 14, 1882, authorizing that of the $20,000 previously voted by Parliament, $18,000 be placed at the disposal of the Hudson's Bay Company to expend on river improvements; the residue was to be retained to cover the cost of Government supervision. This information was not transmitted to Brydges until July 27, and it was then too late to organize work that season.

In his reply, dated August 15, Brydges expressed doubts about the desirability of making improvements to the main river, in view of the expectation that the steel of the Canadian Pacific Railway would touch the South Saskatchewan by the time navigation opened in 1883. This point might become the port

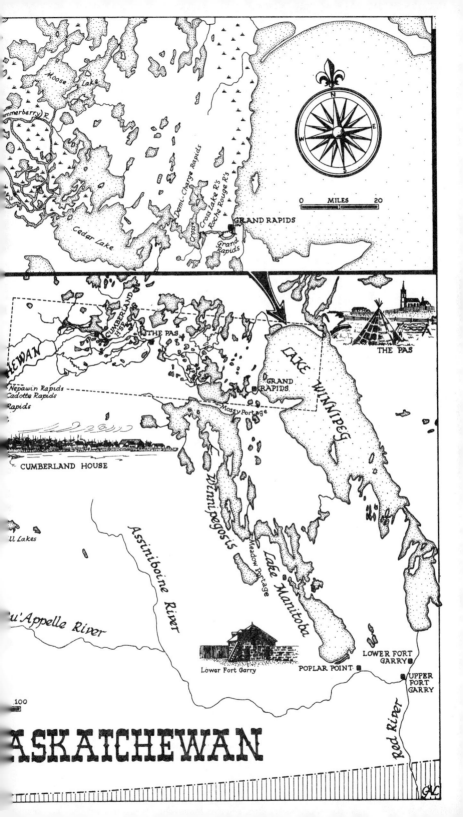

of departure for the steamers supplying the settlements along the north branch, and would mean the abandonment of the lower river. However, in a second letter, of September 27, Brydges wrote that the steamers would use the lower river for two more seasons, so the Company was prepared to proceed with the construction of the pier at the head of the Demi-Charge Rapids, on the understanding that the Government expend money on other river improvements.

Brydges reported to the Department of Public Works on May 4, 1883, that he had engaged a competent man with considerable experience in making improvements on the Mississippi and Missouri rivers to supervise the work on the Saskatchewan. This was Mr. Burbank, probably a member of the St. Paul family engaged in stagecoach and steamboat transportation. He was given the title of Superintendent of Saskatchewan River Improvements.

Superintendent Burbank and his party of fourteen men were unable to reach the Saskatchewan before July, 1883, because the late break-up of the ice on Lake Winnipeg delayed the lake steamer's sailing until June 18. They traveled up the Saskatchewan aboard the **Manitoba,** half the party disembarking at Prince Albert, the other half continuing to Edmonton. At each port the gangs found timber ready for the construction of a scow.

The scow built in Edmonton was described by the local newspaper as being 50 feet by 12 feet. She was equipped to anchor in rapids by the use of two anchors, and two grousers located on either side. She was fitted with a hoisting apparatus extending out over the bow and intended to lift boulders out of the river. She also carried blasting materials to break up boulders too large to lift. A cabin aft provided living quarters for the crew.

The Edmonton scow began work at Point à Pic rock and rapids (also called Stony Rapids) near Fort Saskatchewan, and by freeze-up (November 5) had worked its way downstream another eighty miles to Grahame's Crooked Rapids. The greatest concentration of effort had to be made at Wheeler's Island, seven miles above Vermilion River, and at Victoria Rapids. In each place, about four hundred boulders, ranging in size from 500 pounds to five tons, were removed. At Wheeler's Island the channel was widened to sixty feet and deepened to twenty-two inches at low summer level. At Victoria the channel was changed, and had a depth of thirty-three inches in low water stage. In all, the crew removed or blasted boulders at ten places along the river.

The Prince Albert scow found more than enough work in the numerous rapids of the Cole's Falls series. The scow worked its way about two-thirds of the way down the rapids.

The **Prince Albert Times** of October 3, in an article entitled "Improvement of the Saskatchewan," voiced the dissatisfaction of local people that more had not been accomplished at Cole's Falls, recognized as the most difficult reach of the river. The paper claimed that the dredging scow was too small and light for hoisting boulders. It said the old-fashioned blasting powder method was too slow, and recommended the use of dynamite or nitroglycerine.

Mr. Brydges, in submitting a report on the work completed during the season, stressed the desirability of having a steam-propelled vessel specially built for the task. He said that such a boat should be so equipped that not only could it remove or blast boulders, but it could also drive piles for the construction of wing dams, and dredge channels through sand bars. He suggested that the engine and machinery of the **Lily,** lately wrecked below Medicine Hat, might be used in such a boat, and offered to sell the salvage from the **Lily** for $2,000. Nothing came of this worth-while proposal.

Three years later the **Saskatchewan Herald** complained that little was accomplished in improving the river channel because of the lack of a steam barge:

. . . as here the present barge used by the engineers is not large enough to carry all the stones required to be taken out of the rapids, has not the power to go to the shore when loaded, and is obliged in consequence, to float with the current.

Not being able to return, the work is left half done.[4]

Mr. Brydges submitted accounts showing an expenditure of $14,996.57 on river improvements in the 1883 season.

The following summer, 1884, on July 14, the Burbank party embarked at Edmonton for downstream. The party's first project was to place numbered targets on the points of all the islands as far as the Forks; these markers were to serve as guides to the steamboat men. The party then concentrated its efforts on further improvements in Cole's Falls at the request of the steamboat people. The latter had their most competent pilot go over the series of rapids with Burbank to mark boulders the pilots wanted removed. The work at Cole's Falls was discontinued about October 20. Burbank also made a preliminary survey of the South Saskatchewan River for a hundred miles above the Forks. He listed twenty-eight minor rapids in that distance.

The river improvements in 1884 were again supervised and executed by the Hudson's Bay Company. Mr. Brydges submitted a bill of $8,229.61 to the Department of Public Works.

The disruption by the Riel Rebellion in the spring of 1885 prevented the organization of a river improvement program that season.

In mid-August, 1886, J. B. Williams, an engineer, and Max J. Charbonneau, a Dominion land surveyor, arrived in Prince Albert to undertake a survey of the river down to its mouth. They were reported as collecting boats and supplies, and as not expecting to survey further than the Forks that season.

In the 1888 session of the House of Commons, during the debate on the supply vote which provided $6,000 for Saskatchewan River improvements, Sir Hector Langevin gave the following information in reply to questioning.[5] At Cole's Falls, as of 1887, the first and second rapids at the lower end had been cleared of boulders to leave a channel of three feet in the very lowest stage of water. On the third rapid, a good depth of five feet of water had been found, so no further work had been done. The fourth rapid had

119

COLE'S FALLS: N. Saskatchewan River

After map PUBLIC ARCHIVES

HEAD OF COLE'S FALLS
14 MILES LONG

Rocks

2nd Rapid 600 yards long, Fall 2·5 feet.

Least Water 4'6"
7'6'·5'6'·4'·6'·5'6'

3rd Rapid 500 yards long, Fall 2·0 feet.

3'

4th Rapid 300 yards long, Fall 1·0 foot, Current 3 min. Sept. 14th. 1883

3'6"
3'
3'6'

5th. Rapid 500 yards long, Fall 3·0 feet, Current 3¾ min.

4'6'
5'
4'
4'
4'6' 5'

6th Rapid 250 yards long, Fall 1·0 foot, Currant 1¾ min.

5'
6'
5'

7th Rapid 300 yards long, Fall 0·6 foot, Current 2½ min. Sept 17th. 1883

8'6'·4'26'
4'6'·5'·6·4' 4'6'

8th Rapid 280 yards long, Fall 1·0 foot, Current 4 min.

Rocks

9th Rapid 200 yards long, Fall 1·0 foot, Current 2 min. Sept 21st. 1883.

10th. Rapid 500 yards long, Fall 2·0 feet.
11th. Rapid 275 yards long, Fall 2·0 feet.

Gravel

12th Rapid 450 yards long, Fall 3·6 feet, Current 4 min. Standard water 2½ feet. Oct. 5th.1883.

13th. Rapid 400 yards long, Fall 3·6 feet, Current 2½ min.

Boulders

2'
2' 2'

14th. Rapid 300 yards long, Fall 2·0 feet, Currant 2¼ min. Oct 10th. 1883. 2·0 feet of water and up-
15th. Rapid 450 yards long, Fall 3·6 feet, Current 3 min. 20 inches of water (wards on rapid.

Sand
Swift Water
Rocks

16th. Rapid 200 yards long, Fall 2·0 feet
17th. Rapid 500 yards long, Fall 3·0 feet

18th Rapid
Good depth of water 4' to 6'
Strong Current to the Foot

300 yards long, Fall 2·8 feet
19th. Rapid 700 yards long, Fall 4·0 feet
20th Rapid 500 yards long, Fall 4·0 feet.

FOOT OF COLE'S FALLS

SASKATCHEWAN RIVER

The Forks

South Saskatchewan River

GAC.

been obstructed by boulders but it had been entirely cleared. However, in one place the dredging crew had found it impossible to clear a channel of more than sixteen inches' depth for a distance of about 150 feet, as the bottom was hard gravel and the crew did not have a dredge. Rapid number 5, Little Demi-Charge, one of the worst obstructions and most dangerous on account of the great velocity of water, could not be entirely cleared of boulders because of the great difficulty in reaching them with the stone lifter, and with the limited power at the command of the party. This completed the work of removing obstructions and deepening the channel over the last four of the twenty separate rapids in Cole's Falls. (Burbank's men had worked on the sixteen upper rapids of the series in 1883, and again in 1884.)

The expenditure of public money on river improvements seems to have come to an end in 1888, but by that time everyone realized that the steamboat era was almost over. The Dominion Department of Public Works had spent $60,037.08 to June, 1889, on the Saskatchewan steamboat channels.[6]

An opinion by the steamboat men on the work of the dredgers was given some years later by the crew of the **North West:**

The officers say that the alleged river improvements of a number of years ago were little if any improvement. Instead of the actual boat channel being cleared a great deal of money was expended in making new channels, which, owing to adverse currents, cannot be used, and in some cases rocks or pieces of rocks taken from the proposed impracticable channel have been dropped in the actual channel, thereby impeding instead of assisting navigation.[7]

Chapter 17

NAVIGATION SEASON 1883

IN MARCH, 1883, the merchants of Prince Albert petitioned the Dominion Department of Public Works[1] to remove boulders in the channel of the Saskatchewan so that steamers could ascend the river with their cargoes when the water was in ordinary stage:

> . . . the river, at its normal stage of water, though quite deep enough for purposes of transport, were the channel improved, is yet so obstructed by boulders as to be almost useless; an evidence of which is seen in the result of last year's traffic, when owing to the three new steamers having only surmounted Grand Rapids at an advanced period in the season, they were practically useless, on account of the numerous boulders which obstructed the channel. In consequence, many of our merchants, and, in fact, all classes of the community who had ordered their supplies by steamer, have incurred heavy loss and inconvenience. A large portion of the supplies for Prince Albert, Battleford, Edmonton, and for the Indian Department, is now wintering at Cum-

berland, much of them perishable, and, therefore, likely to suffer great damage. This is an experience which, with the growing traffic, will be yearly repeated, unless some improvement is put upon the river, which is quite capable of improvement at a very moderate expense.

The nineteen petitioners further expressed the view that with the improvements they urged on the Government, the transportation company might be able to reduce its cargo rates by at least forty dollars a ton.

As described in the previous chapter, work on the improvement of the river channel began in the summer of 1883.

With the opening of navigation in 1883 the North West Navigation Company on Lake Winnipeg and the Winnipeg and Western Transportation Company on the Saskatchewan had expectations of a successful season. The **Saskatchewan Herald** bespoke the optimism of the rivermen:

The steamboat companies have their lines fully organized and feel confident to handle all freight that offers, and of making the route a popular one with tourists. The trip presents to the pleasure seeker many points of grandeur and interest —fresh, and free from the hackneyed sameness that characterizes so many of the old so-called pleasure resorts of the East.[2]

The Winnipeg and Western Transportation Company announced the appointment of Captain John B. Davis as commodore of its Saskatchewan fleet. A resident of Rock Island, Illinois, Davis was described as

McPhillips' Alphabetical Directory of Saskatchewan

Prince Albert in 1888. The above view is taken from the bank of the Saskatchewan River. On the right is the North Saskatchewan, which at this point flows due east. The first building on the left is the Roman Catholic mission. The next is the residence of Louis Schmidt, assistant Dominion Lands Agent. To the right of River Street and between it and the river is a cluster of buildings the center of which is the store of Charles Mair. Among them is the Crown Timber office, the residences of Mr. Mair, Mr. Kennedy and Mr. Coombs, Thos. McKay's large storehouse and Jas. Sanderson's sawmill. About half a mile beyond and to the left—(not given in the above view)—stands the cluster of buildings which, in the early days, sprung up on the Porter estate. Still farther on, and to the left, are St. Mary's church, Emmanuel College, and the residences of Mrs. McLean, Thos. Swanston, Ven. Arch-deacon Mackay and Rev. Canon Flett.

an experienced boat officer with thirty-five years of experience in the transport business of the Ohio and upper Mississippi rivers.

Davis's attempt to run a boat over the low watershed from the upper reaches of the Mississippi to the upper Red River was long a legend among the rivermen. In 1859, at St. Paul, he purchased the sternwheeler **Freighter** and took on a cargo for the Red River. He attempted to reach the Red via Lake Traverse and Big Stone Lake, but the season was late and the water falling. The sternwheeler got stuck fast on what was practically dry land ten miles beyond Big Stone:[3]

> Whether the crew drank too much whiskey at New Ulm, or the boat found too little water at the divide, authorities differ; but all agree that the captain and his crew came home in a canoe about the last of July, passing Mankato on the 25th of the month having left his steamboat in dry dock near the Dakota line. The Indians pillaged her of everything but the hull, and that half buried in the sand about ten miles below Big Stone Lake remained visible for twenty or thirty years afterwards. The captain always claimed that if he had started a month earlier his attempt would have been successful.[4]

The machinery of the **Freighter** was salvaged and taken to Georgetown where it was used to power the **Anson Northrup,** first steamboat on the Red River.

Many years later, in 1876, Captain Davis was involved in another steamboat gamble, this time on the Yellowstone River. Acting as agent for William F. Davidson, of St. Paul, he made the low bid on a contract to transport supplies the following season for the American army, then engaged in controlling hostile Indians in the Yellowstone area. Being a Mississippi riverman, Davis failed to take into his calculations the difficulties and hazards of navigating the shallower Missouri and Yellowstone rivers, factors which increased the time and cost of transporting the cargo. The short-lived Yellowstone Transportation Company, in attempting to use Mississippi boat and navigation methods on the shallow Yellowstone, was unable to carry out its commitments. Now, in 1883, Davis was taking charge of the fleet on a river on which navigation was even a bigger gamble than on the American rivers on which he had sailed.[5]

On the Saskatchewan River the plan for 1883 called for the **North West** and the **Marquis** to operate on the lower river as far as Prince Albert, the **Northcote** and the **Manitoba** on the upper river to Edmonton. At Grand Rapids, to assure rapid unloading from the lake steamers **Princess** and **Colvile** and movement over the tramway to the river steamers above the rapids, fifty stevedores were brought from Winnipeg. The **Lily** was to be overhauled and put back into service so that she could be sent on an exploratory voyage up the South Saskatchewan River to Medicine Hat, a new town which the steel of the Canadian Pacific Railway would reach during the summer.

Unfortunately for these well-laid plans, the water in the Saskatchewan River was lower all summer than it had been any year since 1878. Normally the water level rose in June as the melting snow from the Rocky Mountains came down-river, but in 1883 there was no rise because the summer was exceptionally cold and little melting occurred in the mountains. A further navigational difficulty was that below The Cut-Off the river continued to lose its way in new channels and marshes.

Before the spring break-up, Captain Sheets, of the **North West,** left Winnipeg by dog team for Cumberland House. The other captains and the boat crews traveled westward on the new Canadian Pacific Railway to Swift Current where they launched two York boats on Swift Current Creek. Seven days from the mouth of the creek, down the south and main Saskatchewan, brought them to Cumberland House and their boats. Pilot Favell, who had wintered at Victoria Mission, came down-river in a skiff, and met the **North West** above The Cut-Off upward bound; he took over the piloting.

The **North West** took eight days to Battleford, where she arrived on May 15, the earliest arrival on record. She unloaded an immense cargo and several passengers at that point, and continued to Edmonton with 100 tons of freight. The steamboat had a mishap ascending Victoria Rapids when the stern swung around and struck a rock. The impact broke the rudder irons, locking the paddle wheel. The helpless vessel drifted broadside over the rapids. The anchor was thrown out but would not hold. Fortunately, these rapids were among the minor ones in the river, and the boat was not swamped or damaged.

Ernest Brown Collection—Alberta Archives

This photograph of the steamer NORTH WEST evokes the peace and beauty that could be experienced during a trip on the Saskatchewan River when the water was high, the river wide and rocks and sand bars well out of danger and far below.

A reminder that fur production was still an important industry in the Saskatchewan country is found in the cargo carried down-river; at every port of call the steamboat picked up pắckets of fur. She reached Cedar Lake on May 29, where she was delayed for a day because the ice had not yet cleared out of the lake.

The **North West,** while waiting at Grand Rapids for the **Princess,** was overhauled, repainted, and newly furnished.[6] She sailed on June 26 with 196 tons of freight for Prince Albert, which she reached on July 1. She left for Grand Rapids on the 3rd and arrived on the 6th. On her third voyage she sailed for Prince Albert on July 17, and was back again at Grand Rapids on July 28.

On her fourth voyage she sailed on July 30, with 206 tons. Wind caused a delay of two days in crossing Cedar Lake. West of Cumberland she ran into difficulty with shoals, being able to find only two feet of water when she required a draft of four. She turned back to Cumberland, unloaded half her cargo, and tried again. For a day and a half she tried to get through the shoals, but had to turn back and unload the remainder of her cargo at Cumberland.

The **North West** then returned to Grand Rapids, where there was a large amount of freight for Prince Albert and other river ports, but the agent would not release it when the steamer could not guarantee to get it through. With only a hundred bags of flour consigned to Cumberland, she sailed upstream. She arrived at Cumberland House on August 12, and was beached for the winter.

The flag ship of the fleet, the **Marquis,** was under the command of Captain Russell. She sailed from Grand Rapids with 200 tons of freight on July 5, and reached Carlton House without mishap.

The palace steamer took aboard 294 tons of freight at Grand Rapids for her second voyage. She reached the Forks but was unable to climb Cole's Falls and was forced to unload her cargo on the riverbank. On August 1 the **Prince Albert Times** complained that there were several binders aboard and these were needed in the settlement for harvesting the grain crop. This cargo was later moved up by the **Northcote.**

On her voyage downstream the **Marquis** had difficulty finding a channel below The Cut-Off. The ship tried the Sturgeon River channel but was unable to get through. She tried the old channel of the river. Here, the ship's hands had to go overboard with spades to stop up little channels and rivulets in order to raise the water level sufficiently to keep the steamboat afloat. She took nine days to travel from The Cut-Off to deep water. She reached Grand Rapids on August 11, and was laid up for the winter.

The **Northcote,** under the command of Captain Webber, sailed from Cumberland House in mid-May with 2,000 sacks of flour for Battleford and 1,600 sacks for Fort Pitt, cargo for the Department of Indian Affairs. The steamer passed Battleford on May 23, and continued to Frog Creek above Pitt. She passed Battleford going downstream on June 3.

On June 12 the **Northcote** was back in Battleford with another cargo of flour; and equipment and supplies for government survey parties.

On her next voyage up, this time from Grand Rapids, the steamer was plagued by misfortune, caused mostly by the lowness of the water. It took her six days to get over the sand bars between Prince Albert and Battleford.

Sternwheelers operating in shallow waters had a system of spars to help them over the shoals. The appearance and use of the apparatus were aptly described by the Governor General, the Marquis of Lorne, as quoted earlier:

> . . . a curious erection of beams on the forward deck. Two things like the gyns used in lifting heavy weights, are placed on each side. The heavy weight to be lifted in this case is the vessel itself. As soon as very shallow water is struck, two long beams are put over the side, the wheel astern churns up the water, and the ship is fairly lifted on these, as a lame man is on crutches, for a few feet over the obstacle. The poles are then hoisted, and put forward again into the sand, and another step onward is made. Where such a rig is not provided, the only means of making progress consists in getting out a hawser and attaching it to something on the bank. The capstan is then manned and the hawser hauled upon, and with much shouting, rocking of the boat, and convulsive efforts of the engines, step by step, way is gained, until deeper water is reached.[7]

In rapids near Fort Pitt the **Northcote** struck a rock. The deck hands were moving cargo in the hold of the vessel, and fearing that the boat would sink, scrambled for the upper deck. One man in his haste

Public Archives of Canada

Fort Pitt, Hudson's Bay Company.

bumped his head, making a fearful gash. Meanwhile, the captain had ordered the steamer into reverse, and when he saw the boat shipping water, yelled for blankets. When thrown overboard, these stanched the flow into the ship's hold. On arrival at Pitt, one of the steamboat's planks was found to be slightly bulged in.

The **Northcote** was delayed twelve days at Pitt, where she unloaded seventy-seven tons of freight because of the low water. Carrying only forty tons, and drawing thirty-four inches of water, she took seven days to make Edmonton. She arrived on Sunday, August 5.

The water having risen, she returned to Pitt and brought the rest of her cargo to Edmonton. From Edmonton she took 600 bales of fur, and some lumber.

Later, the **Northcote** made two short trips between Prince Albert and the Forks to bring up cargo discharged on the riverbank by the **Marquis.** The **Northcote** was then hauled up on the ways for winter.

The **Manitoba,** in the 1883 season, was under the command of Captain James W. Lauderdale.[8] He had been born in 1844 at Burlington, Iowa, and moved with his family to St. Paul in 1851. He followed the river life as a pilot and captain for a total of twenty-seven years, of which fourteen were spent on the Red River. According to his obituary notice, he was the first to run a steamboat across Lake Winnipeg, which, if the information was correct, would be the **Chief Commissioner** in 1872. Tragedy called Lauderdale from his command of the **Manitoba;** in St. Paul, two of his children died of typhoid fever and he returned home.

The **Manitoba** made one through trip from Cumberland House to Edmonton, which she reached about July 12. She carried cargo which had left Winnipeg on June 18. At Edmonton the passengers, according to the **Bulletin,** spoke highly of the courtesy of the crew, and praised the cabin accommodation and cookery as superior to that of any boat on the river.

Returning to Prince Albert, the steamer took on a full load of freight for Battleford and Edmonton. Some distance above Carlton she found that she could not proceed unless some of her freight was discharged, so she returned to Carlton where she unloaded the Battleford freight. Arriving at Battleford, she had to unload all her freight except some mill machinery for Turtle River.

The steamer, returning downstream, passed Battleford on July 31 and proceeded to Prince Albert. The level of the water rose several inches, and on August 7 the steamer was back in Battleford with a cargo of ninety tons of which thirty-five tons were for that port. She picked up the freight for Fort Pitt which she had unloaded earlier, and sailed on upstream to Edmonton.

The **Manitoba** made her last upward trip from Prince Albert en route to Fort Pitt late in August. She passed Battleford on August 25, and got only twenty-five miles beyond when she struck shoal water. She unloaded part of her cargo, and when she still could not make progress, unloaded all her freight and returned to Prince Albert. Here she was beached for the winter.

Superintendent Davis reported at the end of the

season that the four boats of the line had carried 2,760 tons of freight.[9] However, an analysis of this figure shows that about 500 tons of this consisted of freight stored over winter at Cumberland House, as explained earlier, and perhaps another 700 or 800 tons of freight transshipped on a second steamer on the upper part of the route. Thus, the actual amount of new freight brought into the Saskatchewan country by steamboat approximated the 1,468 tons of the previous year.

Chapter 18

THE LAST VOYAGE OF THE LILY

I N JULY, 1883, the **Lily** was sent up the South
Saskatchewan to test the navigability of that
stream. The steel of the Canadian Pacific Railway
would reach Medicine Hat during the summer, and
the directors of the Winnipeg and Western Transportation Company proposed, if the **Lily's** exploratory
trip were successful, to make Medicine Hat the
port from which the steamers would supply the settlements along the North Saskatchewan.

The iron vessel was placed under the command
of Captain John Scribner Segers, making his first appearance on the Saskatchewan. He had been born at
Bangor, Maine, in 1834, but his family had migrated
to Minnesota in 1853 with a large group of fellow
townsmen who founded several new communities.
The Segers family settled in Henderson, and young
Segers was soon following the life of a riverman on
the Minnesota and upper Mississippi rivers. He seems
to have moved to the Red River in the 1860's where
he was employed on such vessels as the **Anson
Northrup,** later the **International,** and in the mid-
1870's on the **Manitoba** and the **Minnesota.** He was

listed as the captain of the **International** in the 1874 and 1875 seasons. As his subsequent life story will reveal, Captain Segers probably navigated more rivers than any of the great rivermen of the continent. He navigated rivers flowing into the Gulf of Mexico, Hudson Bay, the Beaufort Sea, Bering Strait, and even the Mediterranean Sea.[1]

With Segers as captain, the **Lily** was reported by the **Prince Albert Times,** on June 6, as being repaired and almost ready for launching, but it was July 17 before she sailed.

Taking aboard a large load of cordwood, since much of the trip would be through treeless prairie, she sailed downstream to the Forks, and then turned up the South Saskatchewan. She sailed past the Métis settlements of St. Louis and Batoche. On July 21 she passed the newly established Temperance Colony at Saskatoon and, as the captain jocularly reported, the price of lots in the townsite immediately doubled. Eight days later the steel steamer came upon two scows and a raft of lumber, Saskatoon bound, caught fast on a sand bar.

The crew saw a buffalo bull in the river bottom, surely one of the last buffalo to be seen on the Canadian plains. Once the steamer came abreast of an Indian encampment, and the chief was invited aboard for a cup of tea.

Upon entering the open plains, the crew of the **Lily** had difficulty finding wood enough to keep up steam. At a critical stage in the fuel supply, near the Red Deer Forks, they sighted three log shanties, the winter homes of Métis hunters. The crew dismantled

Public Archives of Canada

Sand bars on the Saskatchewan River.

two houses, and carried off the logs to fire the boilers. What a surprise the owners must have experienced when they returned in the fall expecting to winter in their shanties!

The **Lily** reached Medicine Hat on August 3. She had averaged four miles an hour on her voyage upstream.[2]

She left Medicine Hat on August 29 on her final voyage. The sixty tons of freight were fortunately mostly in the barges she towed. In addition to her own captain, she had aboard the commodore of the line, Captain Davis, and the captain of the **Marquis**, A. R. Russell.

The water had fallen six inches since the **Lily** had come up-river. At Drowning Ford, some forty miles below Medicine Hat, she ran over a submerged rock. Eight feet of her iron plating was torn off the starboard knuckle, and she went to the bottom with all hands aboard—in three feet of water.

The transport company in Winnipeg, upon receipt of a report of the wreck, decided to send an agent to the scene with orders to salvage everything that he could, and to transport the freight back to Medicine Hat; subsequently it was learned that only forty sacks of bacon were damaged by water.[3]

The **Lily** was written off as a total wreck. She was valued at $20,000, and was insured. The General Court of the Hudson's Bay Company was told:

. . . the loss has all been written off and notwithstanding this, we are able to report that there is a profit on our underwriting account for the past year.[4]

Late in 1883, Mr. Brydges, in reporting to the Department of Public Works on the river improvements made during the season, suggested that a steam dredge was required to effectively execute the work. He suggested that the machinery from the **Lily** be put in such a boat.[5] The **Lily's** machinery had been salvaged and piled on the bank, and could be obtained for $2,000,[6] but as late as 1924 parts of the ship might still be seen at Drowning Ford.

Fifty years after the wreck, a Hollywood actor, Clarence H. Geldert, turned up in Saskatoon. He gave an interesting but somewhat inaccurate account of the aftermath of the sinking of the **Lily.** According to his story, he was a youth of seventeen in **Medicine** Hat and had fallen into the bad company of navvies building the Canadian Pacific Railway. The superintendent of the Mounted Police shipped him off aboard the **Lily,** bound for Fort Saskatchewan where his father was working. After the wreck young Geldert came down-river with Captain Davis, whom he recalled as "old man Hoover," and the captain's daughter and son. The shipwrecked party ran out of food, and for a day went hungry. Expecting to see Saskatoon, they kept rowing long after dark. When they decided to camp for the night, Geldert climbed the bank and in the distance saw the twinkle of a light in the village. He was standing on cultivated soil, a potato patch planted by one of the Temperance Colonists. He carried potatoes down to his starving friends, which, in their hunger, they ate raw.[7]

Chapter 19

NAVIGATION SEASON 1884

THE NAVIGATION SEASON of 1884 was a most unprofitable one for the Winnipeg and Western Transportation Company. The level of the water in the vast swamps along the lower Saskatchewan was low from 1883, and these swamps had to fill before the river could be expected to rise perceptibly. The river below The Cut-Off remained capricious. Perhaps an even more serious result of the unsatisfactory 1883 season was that shippers had lost confidence in steamboat transportation; consequently, early in the 1884 season the steamboats were laid up for lack of cargo.

At a directors' meeting held in Winnipeg on March 8 before the season opened, the decision was taken to run only two boats and to employ only two crews.[1] The **North West** would go up-river from Cumberland as soon as the ice went out and then return to Grand Rapids to clean out the freight there. One of the boats wintering at Prince Albert, presumably the **Manitoba,** was to sail up the South Saskatchewan to a point opposite Swift Current and to run from there. These plans were later changed, for all four boats were in operation during the season.

At Cumberland House the **North West** was got into the water early in May. After unsuccessful attempts had been made at sailing her, the boat had to be laid up for nearly a month. Captain Sheets said he had never seen the river so low.

Sketch by S. Hall—Public Archives of Canada

This scene shows a bastion at Fort Carlton as seen by the artist S. Hall in 1881

The **North West** later went down to Grand Rapids and took on cargo. Because of the low water, the steamer had to make two trips with half cargo up the three lower rapids to Cedar Lake. On the second trip up, she found the **Marquis** stuck in the Roche Rouge Rapids unable to move till there would be a rise in water. The **North West** brought 200 tons of freight to Carlton House, which she reached on May 31, and returned to Grand Rapids.

After taking on some cargo she again set out

up-river, picking up cargo which had been left the previous season at various points. The freight which had been left in 1883 at Cumberland was over-hauled, and that for posts above Carlton was taken aboard. The **North West** now had a cargo of 300 tons, of which 100 tons were destined for Battleford, a similar quantity for Edmonton. Ninety tons re-mained in the Cumberland warehouse, intended for Prince Albert; this was later brought up by the **Marquis.**

The **North West's** arrival at Edmonton was de-scribed in the **Bulletin** of July 12:

Shortly after 5 o'clock last Monday evening the people of this town were startled from their usual reverie by hearing the welcome sounds of a steam-boat whistle. To say that most of the town's folk rushed to the bank of the river and looked with delighted eyes, from the dizzy height upon the boat plowing the water of the noble Saskatchewan beneath, is to put it mildly. There was a general stampede to see the favorite steamer North West gallantly making her way up the raging Sask-atchewan to the landing below the Hudson's Bay Company fort, which place she reached at 5:10.

The **Bulletin** noted that some of the freight re-ceived had been shipped from Winnipeg in 1881, and added that "judging from the 'ability' of some of the bacon received it would not stand another steamboat blockade." Captain Davis, superintendent of the line, who was aboard, said that he did not expect the boat to come up again during the season as there was no freight in sight. Going downstream the **North West** carried lumber to Prince Albert.

The boat came up to Battleford late in July. Her last voyage of the season was in August when she went up to Fort Pitt on the 14th, ·and returned downstream on the 18th. The **Saskatchewan Herald** called the vessel "The greyhound of the Saskatchewan," as she had made four trips up from Grand Rapids. Now there was no more cargo.

The **Manitoba**, under the command of Captain Russell, was reported in the **Herald** of July 26 as having arrived in Battleford from Prince Albert after a voyage of seventy hours. She carried 60,000 feet of lumber and 50,000 laths and shingles. This would seem to have been her only trip of the season. There were reports that she would be towed downstream by the **Marquis;** perhaps she had mechanical troubles.

The steamboat company did not intend to use the **Northcote** during the season and offered her for sale to the North Western Coal and Navigation Company, but the offer was not taken up. In July, the decision was taken to float her and send her up the South Saskatchewan to Medicine Hat.[2] During the launching she was sunk, but was refloated. She left late in July on a voyage which is said to have taken seventeen days. The steamer, on reaching the Hat, went into winter berth at the new railway town.[3]

At the end of the navigation season, the Winnipeg and Western Transportation Company decided to retrench because of the unsatisfactory year and the poor prospects for the next season. At a meeting of directors on November 26, a motion was passed abolishing the position of superintendent which Captain Davis held, thus achieving a saving of $4,000 per year. Captain Sheets was to have supervision of the fleet. The first directive given Sheets was to proceed to Prince Albert to make arrangements to better secure the hog chains on the **North West,** and to cut down the cabin of the **Marquis.**[4]

The new president of the transportation company, Joseph Wrigley, informed Chief Factor Clarke, of Carlton House, that only one vessel would operate the next season. The **Northcote** would be brought from Medicine Hat to Prince Albert and laid up. The **North West** would be worked, and if business justified commissioning a second ship, the **Marquis** would be used. He described the **Northcote** and the **Manitoba** as less profitable ships to work.[5]

Chapter 20

SASKATCHEWAN CAPTAINS ON THE NILE

W ITH THE PROSPECT of employment uncertain for the next season, 1885, three of the Saskatchewan River captains accepted an offer from the British army to operate river steamers on the Nile River in Egypt. The rivermen were A. R. Russell, J. S. Segers, and J. Webber. A fourth captain from Red River, Wm. Robinson, led the party; someone said of Robinson that he could steer a sternwheeler up the side of a mountain in the dew.[1]

In the Sudan, two years earlier, a religious fanatic, Mohammed Ahmed, called the Mahdi, had roused the Arab tribesmen to revolt against the Egyptian overlords. General "Chinese" Charles Gordon, a famous British soldier, and former Governor General of the Sudan, was sent to Khartoum to arrange the withdrawal of Egyptian officials and soldiers. In the weeks after his arrival in the city the military situation deteriorated, and Gordon was cut off from retreat down the Nile. The British Government, under public pressure, belatedly organized a relief expedition under the leadership of General Garnet Wolseley.

Public Archives of Canada

Four Western river captains, A. R. Russell, J. S. Segers, J. Webber, and Wm. Robinson. Unfortunately, the names and photos have not been matched. This picture was taken in Ottawa on October 15, 1884, when they were en route to Egypt to run riverboats on the Nile River for the British Army sent to rescue General Gordon at Khartoum.

General Wolseley, in 1870, had led the Canadian militia from Lake Superior to Fort Garry on Red River to dislodge Louis Riel. His experience in reaching the Red River is said to have influenced him in his decision to advance up the Nile rather than to cross the desert from the Red Sea, as advocated by some arm-chair strategists. Wolseley ordered 800 special boats built, and recruited 400 Canadian voyageurs to man them. He also recruited the four river steamboat captains at Red River for service on steamers on the Nile.

The four captains left Winnipeg on October 8. Reaching New York via Ottawa, they embarked on the **Republic** for Liverpool, and there took passage for Alexandria on the **Magdalla.** Captain Russell was the diarist for the party. The ship called at Malta, where the four rivermen visited the catacombs and marveled at the bones of long-dead commanders of the Knights of Malta, seated and wearing their uniforms and regalia of office.

On November 11 the party reached Alexandria and the next day was ordered to the docks where they saw one of the two sternwheel boats they were to navigate. She was of the same type as the former **Lily** of the Saskatchewan, manufactured by Yarrow and Company on the Clyde in Scotland. The ship-building company named its boats after water flowers, and this steamer was the **Water Lily.** A few days later the party took over the boat, with Robinson as captain, Russell as mate, and Webber and Segers as pilots. The boat, towing two barges, made good time up-river for a thousand miles, as far as Wadi Halfa.

149

The **Water Lily** was then engaged in towing barges between Assouan and Wadi Halfa.

Captains Russell and Segers were sent another 250 miles up-river to take charge of another iron riverboat, the **Lotus.** This boat was being assembled above Semna. With Russell as skipper and Segers as mate, she had her trial run on January 1, 1885, and the next day the two rivermen started with her for Dongola, 240 miles up the river. They had to take their boat up seven cataracts, the last of which was fourteen miles long. The most difficult cataract was Tangour, the second of the series. Here, the boat took about five days to get over. One time, the boat was punctured by rock. At one point all the hawsers parted and the boat turned round and started downstream; had it not been that one stern hawser let go on the shore and dragged its whole length on the river bottom, catching among the rocks and thus keeping the boat straight in the current, the boat would have swamped. To mount another cataract it was necessary to have troops dam one of the channels with loose rock in order to raise the water level. The **Lotus** reached her destination, Dongola, on January 31. Captain Russell, in talking to newsmen after his return to Ottawa, said that the upper reaches of the Nile were the worst on which he had ever had experience as pilot though he had been in the business since 1848.

By the time the rivermen from the Canadian West reached Dongola, the outside world had learned that Khartoum had been captured by the Mahdi's forces on January 26 and General Gordon killed. The British military expedition was recalled.

Three of the Western rivermen—(Webber had elected to remain longer on the Nile)—landed in New York on March 10 and next day arrived back in Ottawa. They were said to have been well paid for their services on the Nile, up to $300 per month. Among their souvenirs they would cherish two service medals as members of the Sudan expedition, one issued by Queen Victoria, the other by the Khedive of Egypt.

On the banks of the Saskatchewan, a man who, like the Mahdi, imagined himself a prophet had a few weeks earlier raised the standard of rebellion at Batoche. Captains Russell and Segers had arrived home just in time to navigate riverboats for the military on the South Saskatchewan to help defeat Riel.

Chapter 21

THE COAL FLEET

THE PRESENCE of coal deposits along the high banks of the Belly River in southern Alberta was known quite early. Elliott Galt, who had been in government service in the West, appreciated the commercial potentialities of the rich coal seams and suggested the formation of a mining company to his father, Sir Alexander Galt. Sir Alexander undertook to raise the capital for the enterprise in England, which he did in the winter of 1882-83. English capital made possible the organization of the North Western Coal and Navigation Company in the spring of 1883.

The new company was capitalized at £50,000 sterling. It was financed mainly by publisher William Lethbridge, his partner, the Honorable William H. Smith of the well-known newsstand and bookstore chain, and William Ashmead Bartlett-Burdett-Coutts.[1] The last-named had recently married Baroness Burdett-Coutts, the wealthiest woman in England, and had changed his name to hers. The place names Burdett, Coutts, and Lethbridge in Southern Alberta honor the financiers who provided the capital to start the mining company.

The first mine was opened at the Coal Banks on December 11, 1882. The problem confronting the mining company was to get the coal to market. The Canadian Pacific Railway, then being constructed across the Prairies, would cross the South Saskatchewan River at Medicine Hat, so that the logical solution seemed to be to transport by barge to the railway where some of the coal would be used by the transcontinental locomotives and the remainder shipped to other markets by rail.

Work on the first of the Company's steamers began in the spring of 1883. The difficulties which had to be overcome in constructing the steamer and barges were immense. First, the lumber for the hull of the steamer had to be brought from the new Company's sawmill in the Porcupine Hills, sixty miles west of the Coal Banks. Other materials required had to be freighted by bull team from Swift Current, then the end-of-steel on the Canadian Pacific Railway.[2]

A Missouri River steamboat man, Josephus Todd, was brought in as chief navigational officer for the Company. Todd had originally been a captain on the Ohio River, but after the American Civil War had moved to the Mississippi and Missouri rivers. He was employed on the Missouri by the Northwest Transportation Company in the seasons of 1872 and 1873. Then he joined the new Missouri River Transportation Company, generally known as the Coulson Line, and had a part ownership in some of the boats. He earned recognition on the river for his reliability

153

in moving freight and in handling men. The Company was forced by competition to withdraw from the upper Missouri, and Captain Todd came to Lethbridge.

A brother, Nels, came also, and had charge of construction of the new steamer.[3]

On July 2, 1883, the hull was launched at the Coal Banks, and floated downstream to Medicine Hat to receive her machinery, which had been shipped from Pittsburgh by rail. The hull was 173 feet long and 30 feet in the beam. The boat was a sternwheel paddle steamer with 49.08 horsepower. Her registered tonnage was 201.63; her gross tonnage was 320.04. With her engines installed she drew 18 inches of water.[4] The new vessel was named the **Baroness,** in honor of Baroness Angela Burdett-Coutts.

This lady was the wealthiest woman in England, and a well-known philanthropist. In 1883 she was in her sixty-ninth year. Two years earlier she had startled English society by marrying her secretary, a young American forty years her junior; but December-June weddings ran in her family. Indeed it was such a marriage many years before that had led to Angela being singled out as the sole heir of an immense fortune. Angela was the daughter of Sir Francis Burdett and his wife Sophia, whose father was a wealthy banker, Thomas Coutts. This old gentleman, a few days after the death of his first wife, married the actress Harriet Mellon, who was thirty years younger than himself. Because his family disapproved so strongly of the marriage, he willed all his property to his wife. She, after some years of widowhood, married a man twenty-five years younger, the ninth Duke of St. Albans, the last Hereditary Grand Falconer of England to actually keep the King's falcons. The Duchess of St. Albans favored Angela over her other step-grandchildren and when she died in 1837, left the Coutts estate to Angela. So Angela Burdett, at the age of twenty-three, found herself in possession of an income of $400,000 per annum, which in those days had perhaps three or four times today's purchasing power. Angela lived long to enjoy her fortune, and to use it on worthy causes; she died in 1906.[5]

When the boat, the **Baroness,** was completed at Medicine Hat, it was found that a six-inch copper pipe for conducting steam to the engines was several inches too long.[6] The shipwrights had no proper cutting tool of sufficient size so botched the babbitting of the join, with the result that when the steam pressure got up to 200 pounds to the square inch, steam escaped in clouds. There was some delay before the join was satisfactorily welded.

An account in the **Winnipeg Daily Times** of August 13, 1883, said that the river steamer was "coaling up for her trial run to the mouth of the Belly River."[7] Her maiden voyage was up to the mouth of the Bow River one day, and back down to Medicine Hat the next. She then sailed for the Coal Banks. The **Baroness** was successful in reaching her upper port with the empty barges in tow.

Sir Alexander Galt's recollection of the navigation season was as follows:

"In 1883 we floated barges from the mines early in May, had the highest water of the season on the fifth of July, and I myself went up the river in the Baroness about the tenth of August."[8]

155

Notman collection—McGill University

During a trip to the West in 1884, Montreal photographer William Notman visited Medicine Hat and photographed the MINNOW and the BARONESS docked beside the railway bridge.

Glenbow Foundation

Launching the MINNOW at Medicine Hat, 1884.

157

At this period, little information was available on the flow of the Belly and South Saskatchewan rivers, and certainly it was not appreciated how dependent was the flow on the melting of snow in the mountains. Later observations showed that the water began to rise early in May and by the middle of the month was in good stage. It then reached its crest about June 20 and fell rapidly after the beginning of July.

In the navigation season of 1883 only 200 tons of coal were floated down to Medicine Hat. It was obvious that if transportation were to depend on the short navigational season, the coal company needed more shipping to move coal in quantity to stockpile at Medicine Hat. The company decided to increase its floating tonnage by two new steamers and sixteen additional barges. This shipbuilding activity was carried on during the fall and winter of 1883-84.

The sternwheeler **Alberta** was named in honor of Her Royal Highness, Princess Louise Caroline Alberta, wife of the Marquis of Lorne, the Governor General. This boat was built at Medicine Hat of lumber shipped in, probably from the Minnesota shipyards. She was 100 feet long by 20 feet in width, and had engines of 30.30 horsepower. Her registered and gross tonnage were 85.72 and 150.07 respectively. She was a better towing vessel than the **Baroness.**

The third steamer was more correctly a tugboat. The little vessel, appropriately christened the **Minnow,** was shipped from Winnipeg on a flatcar. She was 75 feet long by 10 feet wide with an engine of only 5.79 horsepower. Originally a sternwheeler, she was later converted to a screw steamer. She was presumably

The ALBERTA under construction at Medicine Hat, 1884.

Glenbow Foundation

built at Rat Portage (Kenora), at that time a boat-building center.

When the navigation season opened in the spring of 1884, the North Western Coal and Navigation Company had three steamers and twenty-five barges ready to transport coal down the Belly and South Saskatchewan. A third Todd brother, Wesley, was brought in to command the **Alberta**. Navigation proved extremely difficult, as Sir Alexander Galt recalled:

> "In 1884 I waited at Medicine Hat for water till after the twenty-fourth of May, and by the twenty-eighth of June our boats and barges were tied up for the season."[9]

In this short space of time, the **Baroness** made nine trips, the **Alberta** eight; the latter took down 500 tons of coal each trip. It was conceded that river transportation was not the answer. The following summer, a narrow-gauge railway was constructed from Medicine Hat to the Coal Banks, now renamed Lethbridge. The railway was completed on August 28, 1885.

The experiences of the ships of the coal fleet during the second Riel Rebellion in 1885 are narrated in the following chapters.

Chapter 22

NAVIGATION SEASON 1885

W HEN THE second Riel Rebellion broke out at
Batoche on the South Saskatchewan in
March, 1885, the river steamers were still in
their winter quarters. Three vessels of the Winnipeg
and Western Transportation Company were in the
Prince Albert area. The previous fall the **Marquis**
and the **Manitoba** had been run into the mouth of the
Sturgeon River, five miles west of Prince Albert. The
North West was drawn up on the bank in the town
itself.

The remaining vessel of this Company's fleet,
the river veteran **Northcote,** had voyaged up the South
Saskatchewan the previous autumn, and was on the
bank at the railway town of Medicine Hat. The three
vessels of the North Western Coal and Navigation
Company, the **Baroness,** the **Alberta,** and the **Minnow,**
were also in winter quarters in the same town.

The military campaign against the Saskatchewan
Métis opened before the spring break-up of the river.
When the river became navigable the steamboats at
Prince Albert were of little use in the Canadian mili-
tia's campaign against Riel, since they were behind

the enemy's stronghold. Later, however, after the victory at Batoche, the **Marquis** and the **North West** saved Canadian militiamen many a weary mile of marching in the campaign against Poundmaker and Big Bear.

Late in March, at Medicine Hat, Captain Sheets began working on the **Northcote** in preparation for getting her into the water. Police Superintendent Herchmer, with a troop of North West Mounted Police, arrived in Swift Current under orders to march north to Battleford, but he could not cross the South Saskatchewan at Saskatchewan Landing as the ice was unsafe. Hearing that the **Northcote** and the three steamers of the coal company were in some danger at Medicine Hat from a band of Cree Indians encamped near the town, he suggested to Major-General Middleton that the police proceed there to protect the vessels and then patrol the river banks as the **Northcote** sailed downstream.[1]

The Mounted Police troop arrived by special train on the morning of March 31, and the Cree across the river hastily broke camp. Superintendent Herchmer placed all his teams and thirty-five men at the disposal of Captain Sheets to get the **Northcote** down the bank and into the water. The task was completed on April 3.

Late the same night Major-General Middleton wired from the front a directive to the Winnipeg office of the Winnipeg and Western Transportation Company asking that a crew be sent at once to man the **Northcote** and start her down the river.[2] Next morning Captains Segers and Russell, with a boat crew, left by train for Medicine Hat. A special train

Glenbow Foundation

The NORTHCOTE sailing from Medicine Hat for the war front, 1885. The ALBERTA and the BARONESS are moored by the far bank.

carried them from Moose Jaw to their destination. On April 9 the **Northcote,** with two barges in tow, sailed for Saskatchewan Landing.

The same evening, a special train arrived in Medicine Hat with Elliott Galt, of the North Western Coal and Navigation Company, and fifty men. The Company's three steamers and twenty coal barges had been chartered by the Department of the Militia.[3]

Now that the South Saskatchewan River was open, consideration was being given to utilizing it for the transport of soldiers and supplies to the front. Major-General Laurie, Commandant of Bases and Lines of Supply,[4] set up headquarters at Swift Current and Saskatchewan Landing. Unfortunately for the success of river transportation, as events were to reveal, the water level was not high enough to make navigation easy.

Lieutenant-Colonel Otter and his command detrained at Swift Current and marched to Saskatchewan Landing, where they arrived at 3 P.M. on April 14. Otter's instructions were to proceed to the relief of Battleford "either by steamer or trail, with as little delay as possible."[5] At the Landing he found that the **Northcote** had arrived a few hours earlier, but the steamers of the coal fleet had not yet left Medicine Hat. As the one steamer could not carry all his men and stores, he decided to proceed by trail. In the crossing of the river some delay was caused by high winds, which buffeted the steamer, but by the evening of April 17 the 230 vehicles of the Battleford Column were on the north bank.

Captain Sheets[6] originally estimated that the

vessel and its barges could take 350 tons of war supplies, but because of the low stage of the water the
cargo had to be reduced. On the 23rd the steamer
left with half of the Midland Battalions, the Field
Hospital corps, Captain Howard and his Gatling gun,
and ammunitions, provisions, and forage badly needed
by Major-General Middleton.[7] The General, after the
Battle of Fish Creek, delayed his march on Batoche
from April 26 to 30, in daily expectation of the arrival
of the **Northcote.** If a major battle were to be fought,
the General wanted the munitions, and also the
medical men and hospital supplies aboard her. The
Northcote, which her captain had estimated would
take four days to reach the front, took fourteen.

Meanwhile, back at Swift Current, Deputy
Surgeon-General Roddick waited anxiously for reports
of the **Northcote's** progress; the medical corps was
urgently needed at the front after the Fish Creek
skirmish. On April 29 a scout brought word that the
Northcote was aground ten miles above the Elbow.
Colonel Dr. Douglas, V.C., set off down-river from
Saskatchewan Landing in a collapsible canoe (which
he named the "Saskatoon" and in which he later
crossed the English Channel). At the same time, Dr.
Roddick went by rail to Moose Jaw and from there
set off by trail for the field hospital at Saskatoon.[8]
On May 1 Roddick passed the Elbow, where a unit of
the Intelligence Corps reported that the **Northcote**
had passed the previous day. The next day the doctor
met Major Bedson, Senior Transport Officer, on the
trail with fifty teams on his way to the Elbow to meet
the **Northcote** and lighten her load. Bedson turned

Glenbow Foundation

This sketch, made in 1885, shows the steamers ALBERTA and BARONESS of the Galt coal company fleet loading near the far pier at Medicine Hat, Alta. Army tents can be seen on the far bank and guards, with tents, can be seen posted at each end of the bridge to guard it against sabotage.

back to Saskatoon, but the steamer had not arrived there. The doctor and the major set off at daybreak along the river in search of the missing vessel and found her stuck on a sand bar five miles above the town. Later in the day the steamer debarked the hospital unit, and continued downstream, reaching Middleton's camp on May 5. During her voyage she had spent more hours aground than afloat; on each shoal the troops aboard had been employed at shifting the cargo between the steamer and the barges to reduce the draft of each to cross the shoal. The steamer had been further delayed when her capstan broke while pulling the vessel over a shoal.

At Medicine Hat, during this time, the coal fleet was being readied for transport service. The tiny **Minnow** arrived at Saskatchewan Landing on April 27, the **Baroness** on May 5, and the **Alberta** at noon on the 6th. The two larger steamers pulled barges. The only explanation for the delay in sailing would seem to have been the low stage of the water. The river rose eight inches on May 1, and an additional sixteen inches the following day. The captains of the three vessels were, respectively, Maloney, Davis, and Todd.

Concerned about the slow passage of the **Northcote,** Major-General Laurie ordered the **Minnow** to steam down-river to the stranded sternwheeler to take aboard the surgeons, the Gatling gun, and munition for the nine-pounders, and to take these forward to General Middleton. The captain of the boat was anxious to tow a barge with ten tons of oats belonging to a half-breed named Gun. Laurie reluctantly gave

Public Archives of Canada

The NORTHCOTE a few days before the Battle of Batoche.

his consent. With its light draft the **Minnow** should have overtaken the **Northcote,** expedited the transport of the medical corps and hospital supplies, and thus saved unnecessary suffering; the **Minnow** did not arrive at Clark's Crossing until after the **Northcote.** In his report, General Laurie was rightly critical of the captain of the **Minnow.** The tug remained under the authority of the military until May 15, but she accomplished nothing more.

The **Baroness** and the **Alberta,** with barges in tow, left Saskatchewan Landing on May 8. The former abandoned her barge about sixty miles downstream, and arrived at the Crossing on May 14. The **Alberta** with her barge docked on the 17th. General Laurie described the officers of these boats as ineffective in the emergency.[9]

Both vessels were later employed as troop transports.

Chapter 23

THE BATTLE OF BATOCHE

THE **NORTHCOTE** served as a gunboat in the Battle of Batoche. On May 7 at Fish Creek in preparation for battle, the **Northcote** took aboard "C" Company of the Infantry School Corps. In addition, she embarked a few ill or wounded officers, a doctor and a medical corpsman, some members of the Transport Service, several residents of the country, and a newspaper correspondent.[1] In a battle, the vessel could muster nearly fifty rifles. Captain Smith of the Infantry School had command of the riflemen, whose battle stations were on the main deck, but Senior Transport Officer Bedson had overall command of the steamboat and the two supply barges the vessel towed.[2] The navigational details were left to the ship's master, Captain Segers; also aboard was his superior officer, Captain Sheets.

At Fish Creek, Captain Haig, R.E., A.Q.M.G., made the vessel defensible against musketry fire,[3] but Captain Smith was not satisfied and next day at Gabriel's Crossing further improved her defences. In his official report Smith made no reference to the planking taken from Gabriel Dumont's stables to

Public Archives of Canada

This historic photo shows a wagon train of the wound ed leaving Fish Creek for Saskatoon in 1885. The hides of freshly-killed steers were tacked over the tops of th e wagon boxes to form hammocks, and canvas over bent willows formed awnings. There were 35 wounded.

armorplate the lower deck with a double casing of two-inch plank. Nor did he mention the removal from Dumont's "stopping place" of a billiard table, which also became a shield for the soldiers aboard. After the rebellion, the billiard table, like the Bremner furs, was to be a source of embarrassment to General Middleton, who was accused in the Canadian Parliament of countenancing pillage.[4] When the battle was joined, it was found that the half-inch wood of the boat's superstructure did not stop bullets. The invalid soldiers in the cabins had to roll out of their bunks and place mattresses and bolsters against the walls. The pilot house was the most exposed position of all, and it was toward this control center that the rebels directed much of their fire.

General Middleton's plan called for the **Northcote** to co-ordinate her progress on the river with the militia's attack from the land side on Batoche. Thus the steamer would create a diversion in the rear while the militia made the frontal attack on the Métis stronghold. With this in mind, Captain Segers had orders to anchor a little above Batoche village. Perhaps a third of a mile further downstream a wire ferry cable stretched across the river, and the captain was warned to keep a lookout for it.

On the morning of the battle, the **Northcote** pulled up anchor at 6:00 A.M. and dropped downriver to within two miles of Batoche, where she waited as instructed. At 7:40 she gave a toot of her whistle, the signal for General Middleton, and went downriver for the co-ordinated attack timed for eight o'clock. But Middleton's column, marching along the

From the Canadian Pictorial & Illustrated War News

The steamer NORTHCOTE running the gantlet at Batoche, May 8, 1885.

trail about a mile from the riverbank, was somewhat delayed, and the **Northcote** found herself going it alone.

From the wooded banks of the river the enemy poured a fusillade of small-arms fire into the vessel, concentrating on the pilot house.[5] The fire was particularly heavy when the **Northcote** came abreast of Batoche itself. According to the master, he was unable to carry out his instructions to anchor because the boat, encumbered by two loaded barges, was unmanageable. Before he knew it, he was upon the ferry cable.

Some of the rebels, under the direction of Gabriel Dumont,[6] lowered one ferry cable just a moment too late to catch the bow of the **Northcote,** but the second one came down and caught the smokestacks low down. The two stacks crashed onto the hurricane deck; for a time there was a danger of the boat taking fire from the stubs of smokestacks. The half-crippled steamer continued downstream for a couple of miles before dropping anchor.

Because of the strong current and the weight of the barges pushing the boat, the anchor dragged for another mile before it caught. The engagement with the enemy had lasted an hour and ten minutes.

When the damage to the **Northcote** was assessed, it was found that in addition to the smokestacks, the skylights were broken and the whistle was down. Two short bits of smokestack pipe were got into place. As the whistle was the means of signaling the boat's position to General Middleton, it too had to be repaired, but the crew refused to go on deck since

Glenbow Foundation

The NORTHCOTE after the Battle of Batoche, in right foreground, her upper smokestacks gone, her pilot house boarded for protection of the pilot. The MARQUIS is behind.

175

enemy snipers were firing from the banks. Finally, on the promise of rewards of fifty dollars apiece, two men of the Transport Division put the whistle back in place.

The military men aboard were anxious to turn back up-river to rejoin battle, but Captain Segers emphatically declined to expose himself again in the flimsy wheelhouse to Métis sharpshooters. So, materials were carried up and the ship's carpenter was set to work nailing thicker lumber on the outside. This drew the attention of rebel marksmen on the bank, and he was wounded in the heel. Next afternoon, Mr. Bedson's men added more planking and made the house sufficiently bullet-proof to satisfy the captain and pilot.[7]

After further councils of war, the decision was made to go down to Hudson's Bay Crossing where the barges would be left and where a supply of firewood could be taken aboard. The steamboat weighed anchor at 6:30 P.M., and reached Hudson's Bay Crossing the following day at 3:00 P.M. Here they found the **Marquis,** which had come from Prince Albert that morning; a contingent of Mounted Police from the Crossing was aboard ready for Batoche.

The following morning, May 12, the two steamers set off upstream. En route, the steering gear of the **Marquis,** damaged by ice earlier in the season, broke down and she had to be taken in tow by the **Northcote.** The two steamers reached Batoche at 8 P.M., to find that earlier in the day the village had fallen to the Canadian militia.

Captain Smith, in his report, blamed the poor

showing of the **Northcote** in battle on the fact that the master, pilot, and engineer were aliens, and the crew were civilians. In defence of the chief officers of the boat, it must be pointed out that they occupied the most exposed part of the boat, the pilot house, and as aliens it was natural that they should show a disinclination to be killed in another country's war. It was poor naval strategy for a river boat to go into battle with barges in tow, thus reducing maneuverability. Had the **Northcote** anchored just above Batoche, close enough to engage some of the enemy and be a continuing threat to the rear of their lines, the Battle of Batoche might have been short and decisive.

Chapter 24

TROOP TRANSPORTS

W HEN NAVIGATION opened in the spring of the rebellion, there were three sternwheelers in the Prince Albert area. The **North West** was on the riverbank in the town, while the **Marquis** and the **Manitoba** were wintering just inside the mouth of the Sturgeon (or Shell) River, about five miles above the city.

The ice on the Saskatchewan began to move on April 9-10, and went out with some force, for the water was high and the ice flow heavy. Inside the mouth of the Sturgeon, the **Marquis** rose up with the water, but the **Manitoba** remained frozen to the bottom. Ice piled up to a height of twenty feet, burying the **Manitoba**. She was a total wreck. Her value was estimated at $35,000.

The **Marquis** had suffered damage, for her rudders were frozen in the ice and all her hog chains broken. She lay at a 45-degree angle, full of water. A crew, sent out from Prince Albert, repaired the boat's upper hog chains, sawed off three of the four rudder posts, siphoned the water out of her, filled her boilers, and got up steam.[1]

Captain Julius Dougal backed the **Marquis** into the Saskatchewan River. Since she had scarcely any steering apparatus left, it was a wonder that the crew got her going in the right direction, but with a line to hold the stern, they were able to point her downstream. Somehow the captain managed to dock her in Prince Albert. The next day, with block and tackle, the stern of the **Marquis** was pulled out of the water, and carpenters set to work repairing the rudders. In this they were not altogether successful, for her steering apparatus broke down on the voyage to Batoche.

Once repaired, the ship was guarded at night by a patrol of the Prince Albert Volunteers.[2] There were Indians of uncertain loyalty camped across the river who might attempt her destruction. Had the straggling town been seriously threatened by attack, the women and children would have been put aboard the **Marquis** and evacuated to the lower Saskatchewan.

The **Marquis** left Prince Albert on Friday, May 1, for Hudson's Bay Crossing on the south branch. Here thirty-three Mounted Police were protecting four scows and the same number of rowboats. The story of the **Marquis's** meeting with the **Northcote** at the Crossing and of her broken rudders has been narrated. Her steering gear was again repaired, and she served as Middleton's flag ship in the voyage up the north branch to Battleford and Fort Pitt.

Earlier in the season, Captain Sheets had been designated commander of the **North West,** but the rebellion and Major-General Laurie prevented him from joining his ship in April. He had been about to leave Saskatchewan Landing by wagon in the wake

179

of Colonel Otter's Battleford Column, with the idea of going by rowboat from Battleford to Prince Albert, when General Laurie stopped him. The General insisted that Sheets accompany the **Northcote.** Sheets argued that Trade Commissioner Wrigley of the Hudson's Bay Company wanted him to take charge of the **North West** at once; Laurie wired Wrigley and obtained his permission for the captain to sail aboard the **Northcote.** Thus Sheets was not a willing passenger.

No sooner had Sheets got behind the battle lines at Hudson's Bay Crossing than he set off to reach his ship. He sent a delayed telegram to Wrigley in Winnipeg:

> Humboldt, May 13. I leave for Prince Albert to bring steamer North West here. Good water; awaiting fighting orders from General.

The **North West** was given a quick overhaul and a new coat of paint. On a trial run she went up to the mouth of the Sturgeon River to pick up the salvage from the ill-fated **Manitoba.** The **North West** was ready to transport troops when Middleton's Column reached Prince Albert.

Meanwhile, from the battlefield of Batoche, the **Northcote** carried the wounded to the field hospital at Saskatoon. She arrived on the afternoon of May 14, but a violent rain storm prevented the disembarkment of the wounded until the following morning.

Five days later, the **Northcote** came back to Saskatoon with an illustrious prisoner, none other than Louis Riel, the man with Messianic dreams. The

180

rebel chief spent the night under heavy guard aboard the river steamer. Next morning, Riel and his military guard set out by trail for Regina where he would be held prisoner until his trial and execution.

The captain of the **Northcote** was under orders to place his ship at the disposal of Deputy Surgeon-General Roddick for the transport of the wounded. On the evening of May 20 those soldiers well enough to travel were made comfortable in the staterooms and saloon. There were twenty-nine wounded men on the voyage up the river to the Elbow, which was reached on May 23. Here vehicles were waiting to move them to the base hospital at Moose Jaw.

General Middleton was pressing the campaign along the North Saskatchewan against the Indian chiefs Poundmaker and Big Bear. The **Northcote** and the **Marquis** were put into service to transport Middleton's Column across the river at Gardepuy's Crossing on May 16-17. Middleton, with half his force, boarded the waiting **North West** at Prince Albert for Battleford on May 20. Two days later, the 90th Battalion and 10th Grenadiers under the command of Van Straubenzie left Prince Albert on the **Marquis** and the **Alberta**. The cavalry and artillery moved by trail toward Carlton Crossing. At the burnt ruins of Fort Carlton, the troops aboard the **Alberta** were transferred to the **Baroness**; the **Alberta** remained at the Crossing to ferry the mounted troops across so that they could take the shorter north trail to Battleford. The **North West** with General Middleton arrived at Battleford on May 24, the **Marquis** on the evening of May 27. By the time the **Marquis** arrived, Poundmaker had surrendered.

Public Archives of Canada

The first expedition for the relief of Battleford attacked by rebels.

Big Bear was still on the warpath near Fort Pitt further up-river. On May 28 Inspector A. Bowen Perry of the Mounted Police arrived in Battleford with information on the location of Strange's Column advancing down the North Saskatchewan. Early next morning the **North West,** laden with supplies for Strange, and carrying a detachment of Mounted Police and a company of the 90th Rifles, set off up-river. At 4.30 P.M., the steamer met a canoe with a courier who informed them of the engagement between Strange's Column and Big Bear's Cree at Frenchman's Butte. Chief Transport Officer Bedson, who was in command, landed the police detachment, and ordered the boat to turn about and make full steam for Battleford.

General Middleton hastily embarked his force (except the mounted men) aboard the **Marquis,** the **North West,** and the **Baroness,** and sailed northwestward. The purpose was to cut off Big Bear's escape and decisively defeat him. But Big Bear had fled northward into marshy country where it was difficult for troops to follow.

The **North West,** on either her first or second trip, carried the arms surrendered by Poundmaker's warriors. The following account of the disposal of the weapons comes from the memoirs of Archie Ballantine, who was night watchman aboard the sternwheeler that summer:

> They were piled on our boat, the North West and they made a great pile of junk—the old flintlocks red with rust and about six feet long. Very few of the guns were of any value. After

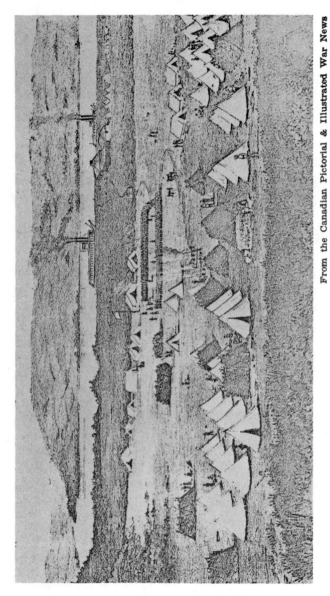

From the Canadian Pictorial & Illustrated War News

Corporal E. C. Currie of No. 4 Company, 10th Battalion, Royal Grenadiers, made this sketch of a church parade held at Fort Pitt on the Sunday morning of June 2, 1885.

the surrender we passed up river and next day pulled into Pine Island, about 90 miles above Battleford, to wood up. The old guns were in the way, so the whole bunch was dumped into the river. We should have kept them for souvenirs to show what we were fighting against.[3]

While Middleton and Strange marched about in the bush, the steamers idled off the ruins of Fort Pitt. During this time, the **Alberta** made two trips to Edmonton, on her first voyage carrying the flatboat men who had accompanied Strange's Column. On June 25, she left Pitt with Chief Factor MacLean and his large family; they had been prisoners of the Wood Cree. The **Baroness** also voyaged up to Edmonton.

By the beginning of July, the military campaign was over. The troops embarked at Fort Pitt for the homeward voyage aboard the **Marquis,** the **North West,** and the **Baroness.** On July 5, the flotilla reached Battleford, on the 8th, Prince Albert, and the same evening the Forks. Here the **Alberta,** with the remainder of the wounded from the Saskatoon field hospital, had been waiting for three days.

The **Alberta** presented a strange appearance with her cluster of barges. On one side was a double barge carrying a company of the Midland Battalions picked up at Clark's Crossing, the hospital barge on the other, and a third barge in front, loaded with cordwood and carrying two cows to supply milk for the sick. The hospital barge had been specially prepared to accommodate twenty beds, and was canopied with canvas. The wounded were carried in the barge to save them any discomfort from the jolting of the steamer's machinery. The **Alberta,** thus encumbered, was slower than the other boats, but each evening Middleton's flag ship, the **Marquis,** slowed down to let her catch up. At Cedar Lake the wounded were transferred to the **Marquis,** as the weather was cloudy and a light southwest wind was blowing. If the wind got up, the lake was dangerous for a small steamer.

Some of the boats called at Cumberland House, where Chief Factor Belanger gave them a salute with his ancient cannon. The **North West** arrived at Grand Rapids at 5:00 P.M. on July 10, carrying the 65th Battalion. The **Marquis** arrived at 5:00 P.M. on the 12th with General Middleton and his staff, the wounded, and the 90th Battalion. The **Marquis** went back across Cedar Lake to take off the rest of the troops from the **Alberta's** double barges. On July 13 at 11:10 A.M. the lake steamer **Princess,** towing the barge **Nelson River,** also loaded with troops, left the lower dock for the voyage across Lake Winnipeg. The **Colvile,** with the barges **Saskatchewan** and **Red River,** let go right afterwards. The town of Selkirk on Red River was reached on July 17.

The last troops along the North Saskatchewan, members of the Winnipeg Light Infantry, were picked up by the **Northcote** in late July. One company had been in garrison at Fort Edmonton, the others guarded thirty Indian prisoners at Pitt. The following is a description of the embarkation at Edmonton:

The 7th Co. of the W.L.I., in garrison at Edmonton for the past two months, left on Sunday. At 11 a.m. the Co. was formed up in the fort in marching order, and presented a fine appearance

186

The lake steamer PRINCESS, a sidewheeler, with the barge RED RIVER at the mouth of the Saskatchewan River. An engraving from a photograph taken by the Otto Klotz party in 1884.

Tuttle. C. R.: Our north land

as they came down the hill at a swing step to embark for home. As the boat turned out into the stream they were given cheer after cheer, hearty and heartfelt, from the large crowd on the bank which had assembled to see them off. The Edmonton amateur field battery fired a salute of five guns from one of the Hudson's Bay Company's brass four pounders, and as the boat passed along, groups on the bank cheered themselves hoarse, to whom the red coats heartily replied.[4]

Peace had been restored along the Saskatchewan.

What Riel's second rebellion meant in revenue to the Saskatchewan river steamers is set out in the Report of the Auditor General of Canada for 1885-86:

North West Coal and Navigation Company: advances	$20,000.00
Winnipeg and Western Transportation Company:	
Steamer Marquis—April 23 to July 12, 81 days at $250	$20,250.00
Steamer Northcote—April 7 to June 12, 67 days	16,750.00
Steamer North West—May 12 to July 12, 62 days	15,500.00
Transport of Winnipeg Light Infantry Fort Pitt to Battleford	1,385.50
Demurrage of Northcote at Fort Pitt	1,000.00
Damage of Northcote at Batoche	950.00
Use of barge, April 7 to May 12, 36 days at $15	540.00
Transport of baggage at Grand Rapids	141.00

Lumber and nails	132.00
Conveyance of man and stores	24.30
	$56,672.80
Less reduction of claim	−3,038.00
	$53,634.80

Chapter 25

RETURN TO COMMERCIAL SERVICE

THE **NORTHCOTE** went back into commercial service on June 12, and four days later was waiting at Grand Rapids when the lake steamer **Princess** arrived. The riverboat started upstream with one hundred tons of freight on June 20, but made slow progress. Off Fort à la Corne, the pump, which had been punctured in running the enemy's fire at Batoche, gave out and had to be repaired. At Battleford, the river was so low that the **Northcote** had to unload forty tons. The water level rose when she was some miles above and she reached Edmonton in mid-July. She then went back to Battleford for the rest of her cargo.

The **North West** left Grand Rapids on July 14 with 218 tons of freight and reached Edmonton sixteen days later. Of the freight, 160 tons were for Edmonton, and three-quarters of this was for the Hudson's Bay Company. On Saturday evening, August 1, Commissioner Wrigley had a dinner party aboard the vessel at the Edmonton wharf.

The Wrigley dinner aboard the **North West**, as remembered by Archie Ballantine, was a gala affair.

A trestle table ran the length of the 120-foot saloon, with dinnerware of all sorts, including trays of birch bark. Gay Hudson's Bay blankets covered seats and benches. Bracket lamps hung from the center of the cabin, casting a yellow glow over the scene. The guests, about eight o'clock, trooped down the hill from the fort and took their places. After dinner, each person in turn recited, sang, or told some tale of adventure. The end man was John Gordon, and he did the Scottish sword dance to the accompaniment of skirling bagpipes. Meanwhile, down on the lower deck, the Company's servants sat in a large circle with plenty of food and kettles of steaming tea. These were the men who had manned the York boats and worn the pack straps, and as they sat they chatted and told stories of the buffalo hunt and the long portage. At midnight, after singing Auld Lang Syne, the guests walked down the gang-plank and dispersed up the hill. The **North West** dropped down to the lower mill to load lumber and at 2:00 A.M. steamed off downriver.

About fifty miles below Edmonton, she broke her hog chain braces crossing a shoal. When the sternwheeler came to the shallow, the pilot rang the slow bell, but the engineer gave her full speed ahead. The river bottom in a shallow can be ridged like a washboard. With the spurt of speed the bow of the boat was pushed lower into the water. As the **North West** had little cargo, all the strain hung on the hog chain braces. The washboard jolting caused the rods to snap and so the vessel humped in the center; the weight of her machinery, located fore and aft, pulled down the bow and stern. The water lines to the boilers and to the whistle in the dome were severed, and escaping steam hissed in all directions. The crew dampered the fires under the boilers as the water ran out.

When the night watchman, Archie Ballantine, woke in late afternoon, he found that the crew had been unable to make the repairs and that the captain had picked out a man to run to Edmonton to bring a blacksmith. Ballantine had had some blacksmithing experience and volunteered his services. He set up trestles on either side of a forge to support the broken rods. Four men on each side of the forge handled the rods and two more kept the bellows blowing mightily. When the broken rod ends were heated to the right degree, they were pushed onto the anvil and beaten together. It took an hour to weld each of the first three rods, and three hours to repair one on which the ends had been damaged when the crew tried to repair it.

With the other breaks temporarily repaired, but still humped like a camel, the **North West** went limping down to Prince Albert. At this port she was hauled up on the bank by blocks and tackles pulled by seven teams of horses. After that, numerous jack screws and blocks and tackles were used to straighten the ship and adjust her hog chains.

The water had risen, and the **North West** made good time going down to Cumberland House. Here, she was laid up for some time waiting for the **Marquis** to arrive from Grand Rapids. The **Marquis** had had to wait for the lake steamer delayed by a storm on Lake Winnipeg, and was herself delayed two days by winds on Cedar Lake. When she arrived at Cumberland House, her cargo was transferred to the "Greyhound of the Saskatchewan."

The **North West** had been using the old channel below The Cut-Off all summer, as the water was in good stage. This time Captain Sheets was not sure that his boat could get through but he decided to try, since it was much shorter than the Sturgeon River route. The boat had gone only three boat lengths in the old channel when she found the water had turned shoal. The deck hands leaped overboard and waded about but could not find deeper water. They had to warp her over the shallow. Fortunately, from then on the boat had little difficulty reaching her destination, Prince Albert.

The last reference to the **North West** to appear that season in the **Prince Albert Times** was on September 25. The newspaper said that the sternwheeler had left the previous morning for Grand Rapids, carrying the crews of the several boats. She did not make Cumberland House, for she was caught in low water in the Sturgeon River channel.

Chapter 26

NAVIGATION SEASON 1886

THE NAVIGATION SEASON of 1886 opened full of promise for the Winnipeg and Western Transportation Company, but ended a dismal failure.

Early in May, Chief Factor Belanger, of Cumberland House, brought the news up to Prince Albert that the three ships of the line, the **Marquis,** the **Northcote,** and the **North West,** were being repaired and would leave Cumberland for Grand Rapids about June 1. With new reductions in freight and passenger rates, Commodore Sheets expected a rush of business.

The **North West,** on her last voyage the previous autumn, had been caught in the shallows of the Sturgeon River, and was in danger of being destroyed by the spring ice. In March, Captain Sheets and a crew of engineers and carpenters arrived by dog team at Cumberland. They erected protective piers around the sternwheeler. However, when the spring break-up came, most of the ice piled on the sand bars and banks of the Saskatchewan River between Fort à la Corne and The Cut-Off. Little ice came down the Sturgeon River channel, and the **North West** was unharmed.

The **North West** reached Grand Rapids on June 2. When she again set off up-river, she carried 250 tons of freight and twenty-five passengers. The boat had difficulty getting up the Demi-Charge Rapids because of low water, but she met a rise in the water level at Cedar Lake. She reached Prince Albert on June 26, and Edmonton on the morning of July 5. The steamer left Edmonton carrying $250,000 worth of furs for the Hudson's Bay Company.

On her second voyage, she sailed from Grand Rapids on the 18th with a cargo of 250 tons. She landed 50 tons at Carlton, 15 at Battleford, 40 at Pitt, 40 at Victoria, and 100 tons at Edmonton. She reached the upper port on August 8.

The **North West** arrived in Prince Albert on her last upward voyage on August 24, en route for Battleford, where she landed 150 tons, and then went into winter quarters at Prince Albert.

The **Marquis,** on her first voyage of the season up the Saskatchewan, reached Prince Albert on July 3, under the command of Captain Julius Dougal. She carried 250 tons, mostly freight for the Hudson's Bay Company, and loaded 100,000 feet of lumber for Battleford.

She also took aboard the town's fourteen - piece cornet band and a party of fifteen excursionists for the voyage to Battleford, which she reached on the second morning out. The boat docked and the band marched up the street of Battleford, entertaining the surprised citizenry. That evening, to quote the **Saskatchewan Herald:**

The spacious cabin of the Marquis having been

placed at the band's disposal by Capt. Dougal, they courteously invited a number of ladies and gentlemen to spend the evening in the enjoyment of a dance.

The **Marquis** went down-river to Grand Rapids where she loaded 168 tons of cargo, and on July 20 started up in company with the **North West.** After unloading cargo at Moose Lake, The Pas, and Cumberland, the **Marquis,** with 97 tons in her hold, arrived at the foot of Thorburn Rapids on July 26 at 5:30 A.M.

The Thorburn Rapids were three-quarters of a mile in length with a current of six miles per hour. The river was crooked, and it was not possible to see the top of the rapids from the lower end. The **Marquis** proceeded up and was almost through the roughest part when she rubbed a rock on her starboard knuckle, which caused her to swing to the right and drift down broadside to the current. She struck on a rock under the forward end of her boilers on the starboard side of her keelson, which knocked a hole through her. The force of the current pivoted her on the rock until her bow faced upstream.

Inspection of the hold showed a rock protruding about a foot into the boat and water pouring in. The crew tried to lift the boat with both spars but could not move her, and she settled back down. Within half an hour her hold was full of water.[1]

The underwriters hired Peter McArthur, of Winnipeg, who had built the **Marquis,** to go to the scene of the wreck to repair the damage.[2] McArthur was to be paid the sum of $20,000. With a gang of thirty-five men he left Winnipeg for Qu'Appelle, and from this railway station all the equipment, except the timbers needed, was trailed by wagon to Prince Albert. Then the party went down-river in scows, leaving the settlement on September 28. Commodore Sheets accompanied the party.

At Thorburn Rapids the water had fallen so low that the men could work dry-shod around the wreck. First the quarryman, Jim Young, removed the boulder. Then the 475-ton vessel was jacked up, and hauled up a slipway to a bench thirty feet above the water level. Horse-operated capstans and rope falls were used in this work. The **Marquis** was almost in place when trouble developed. The ten sets of tackle were under strain, so a foreman had the idea that the bow line was dangerously taut and eased this line off a bit. This placed added strain on No. 2 line, and it snapped, and in a trice all the lines gave way. The boat slid back down the slope, and six weeks' labor went for nothing. Now, the **Marquis** not only had a hole in her hull where she had gone on the rock, but her main steam pipe and her hog chains were broken. The discouraged crew jacked her up again and left her for the winter.

During the 1886 season, nothing had been seen on the upper river of the veteran sternwheeler, the **Northcote**. Captain Jerry Webber, after an absence of two years, was back on the Saskatchewan and skippering the **Northcote;** he had been a member of the party of Canadian boatmen who had volunteered for service under General Wolseley in his campaign up the Nile to the Sudan. But the cataracts of the Nile were not

The NORTHCOTE'S *boilers at Cumberland House.*

so frustrating as the shoals of the Saskatchewan. The **Northcote**, drawing slightly more water than the other boats, was unable to get over the shoals in the many channels of the Sturgeon River route above Cumberland Lake.

The **Saskatchewan Herald** reported on the problem of navigation below The Cut-Off that season. Here, two-thirds of the river's water flowed out, leaving the main river for fifty miles useless for navigation. The water which spilled into the swamp entered Cumberland Lake through a number of channels, but none of them had sufficient depth for the boats. In consequence, the upper boats could not get down nor the lower boat, the **Northcote,** up.

The **Herald** said editorially that it was the opinion of the rivermen that if piles were driven down across the new channel at The Cut-Off, brush and mud would gather and stanch the flow of water out of the main channel. Government action was needed.[3]

Earlier in August, a Dominion Government team of surveyors, J. R. Williams and Max J. Charbonneau, had arrived at Prince Albert to survey the Saskatchewan down to Grand Rapids. Their main concern, however, was with the removal of boulders from rapids, and meanwhile, the life blood of river transportation, the navigable water, was oozing into a swamp.

The **Prince Albert Times** of August 20 reported the arrival of part of the **Northcote's** crew, discharged because of the old veteran's inability to navigate the river.

The **Northcote** was beached at Cumberland House, never to sail again. She slowly disintegrated over the years until nothing but her boilers remained.

The Board of Directors of the Winnipeg and Western Transportation Company, in their annual report, said that the most serious interruption to their business had been the extremely low water, the lowest in years, and the difficulties at The Cut-Off. Freight rates had been lowered because of competition from freighters carrying goods by cart and wagon northward from the stations of the newly completed Canadian Pacific Railway.[4]

At Cumberland 300 tons of freight remained all winter in the warehouse.

Chapter 27

NAVIGATION SEASON 1887

IN THE LATE AUTUMN of 1886, the wrecked **Marquis** had been left at Thorburn Rapids, on jacks, after she slid down the embankment during salvage operations. Early in the spring, the salvager, Peter McArthur, with ten picked men returned to the scene.[1] One of the men was a noted blacksmith, a Glasgow Scot, by name Geordie Munsden. Munsden brazed the fractured steam pipe and repaired the hog chains, but one truss rod defied his best efforts to weld it.

The truss rod was an iron bar 42 feet long with a diameter of 2 inches; it weighed 700 pounds. Without it, the sternwheeler could not navigate. Munsden proposed that it be taken to Prince Albert where a large forge would be available. He and a couple of crewmen got into a rowboat, balanced the two pieces of broken rod across the gunnels, and rowed 160 miles upstream.

At Prince Albert the local blacksmith successfully welded the rod, but when it was being carried down to the riverbank it again broke. Munsden and his men loaded the two pieces aboard their clumsy rowboat and rowed back to the wreck.

Hudson's Bay Company Library

The Grand Rapids tramway as seen and photographed about 1888.

Geordie Munsden had learned a trick or two about welding at Prince Albert and so he prepared another attempt to weld the obstreperous iron. He rigged up supports for the two long rods, built a good fire, instructed his helpers, and set to work heating the broken ends.

The critical moment approached. A few hearty blows with the sledge hammer, and the rod was welded. The men gave three cheers for the smith, and then sat down to a delayed dinner in the dining saloon of the **Marquis.** While they were still at table, a whistle blew, and it was a small steamer with the underwriter's inspector, together with the owner's crew, ready to inspect and take over the vessel.

The **Marquis** did not get beyond Cole's Falls that season, for a report in mid-July said that the **North West** was going to drop down below the Falls to take off her cargo. There was not enough water on the series of rapids to float this biggest of the steamboats. A month later, the **North West** was reported en route to Cumberland Lake to take off the **Marquis's** cargo, as now she could not get above that point.

In the navigation season of 1887, the **North West,** on the other hand, was very successful in navigating the river. Early in May, at her winter berth in Prince Albert, she was caulked and repainted. Perhaps the secret of her success lay in a report that Captain Sheets had discovered a new steamboat channel through the swamp below The Cut-Off which "removes the danger of steamers being blocked at this point."

The steamer went down to Grand Rapids early in

June. She sailed with a heavy cargo at 4:00 A.M. on June 24. At Cedar Lake she was detained by high winds; windows of the pilot house were blown in and the boat was driven aground. Above Carlton she had difficulty as the water level was falling and she was often aground. At Crooked and Sucker Rapids she had to use the line to get up. She reached Edmonton on July 14 with 213 tons of freight. Her arrival was about two weeks later than usual.

On the return voyage the steamer took aboard 151 packets of fur from Edmonton, 37 from Victoria, and 33 from Pitt.

The **North West's** next assignment was to drop down to the Forks to take on the freight left by the **Marquis** when she was unable to climb Cole's Falls. She started back up the Falls on the 23rd. After getting over the first rapid, the Crooked, she had to unload her deck cargo because of the low water. On Tuesday, the 26th, she was forced to unload all the flour in her cargo, and some other freight. On the 27th she broke her wheel several times. She reached Prince Albert on the 28th and unloaded her remaining cargo, then returned down Cole's Falls to pick up the freight she had dropped. She started up on July 30, got safely over Cole's Falls and arrived in Prince Albert at 4:30 P.M. She reached Edmonton on August 2, carrying forty tons of cargo.

From Edmonton, the **North West** went down to Cumberland to pick up the freight left there by the **Marquis.** She was back in Edmonton at the end of August, and then went back down to Cumberland. On her fourth voyage up in mid-September, she could

Manitoba Archives

*The remains of the Hudson's Bay Company tramway at Grand Rapids
as photographed under snow in 1961.*

not climb Cole's Falls and returned to Cumberland to winter. She had moved 674 tons of freight into the country.

Commenting on the unsatisfactory financial report of the directors of the Winnipeg and Western Transportation Company for the year 1887, Trade Commissioner Joseph Wrigley wrote as follows:

The loss on the operating account on the year's business is chiefly caused from only one half the usual amount of freight having been carried. This arises from the indisposition of shippers to send freight where there is great doubt as to the time of delivery caused by the uncertainty of the water in the river. Under present circumstances I fear this uncertainty of water may prove an insuperable obstacle to the success of the Company.[2]

Chapter 28

NAVIGATION SEASONS 1888, 1889, & 1890

IN THE NAVIGATION SEASON of 1888, the
North West was the only steamer of the Winnipeg and Western Transportation line still in
operation. She sailed from Grand Rapids on June
24 with 227 tons aboard. The freight was consigned
for Edmonton by the Hudson's Bay Company to be
transshipped to the Athabasca country. On her second
voyage the steamboat came up to Onion Lake (above
Pitt) with supplies for the Department of Indian Affairs. Late in August the North West was up as far as
Battleford.

Running down Cole's Falls on her first down
voyage, the boat damaged between seventy-five and
one hundred of her floor timbers, but this did not
seriously delay her and repairs were made while she
was under way. Captain Sheets recommended that
the timbers in the forward part of the hull be replaced, as they had worn thin over the years. This
recommendation was not effected until the winter of
1889-90.

The annual report of the Winnipeg and Western
Transportation Company said of the North West:

[she] . . . was kept continuously on the move, and in spite of the capriciousness of the River Saskatchewan was enabled to distribute all the freight coming to hand to its destination.

By strictest economy in every branch, the directors were able, the report said, to present a "not unsatisfactory statement under the circumstances."[1]

The story of the navigation season of 1889 can be told in one terse sentence: there was no navigation. The previous winter's snowfall in the mountains was unusually light, so the river remained low after the spring break-up. Furthermore, no rain fell from May to August along the North Saskatchewan. A Battleford dispatch in mid-July said that the water in the Saskatchewan and Battleford rivers was very low, and concluded by saying, "Navigation is a thing not to be thought of unless present circumstances change."

The **North West** made several attempts to go down-river below Cedar Lake Narrows to Grand Rapids. Finally, the freight had to be brought up by York boat over the Roche Rouge and Demi-Charge rapids to the waiting steamer. The **North West** brought the freight to Cumberland House, but could not navigate beyond. On July 26, the **Prince Albert Times** recorded that the water had slowly risen in the past few days but that it would need to rise a foot or more before steamers could run on it.

In mid-August the steamer's skipper, Captain J. H. Smith, arrived in Prince Albert, having come overland to ascertain the condition of the river. He said that Cumberland Lake was so low that weeds were growing around the shore a quarter of a mile out,

Public Archives of Canada

The MARQUIS *as she appeared in the winter of 1898-99 at Prince Albert. This photo was originally published in the Hudson's Bay Company journal* THE BEAVER, *June, 1943.*

and Thorburn Rapids had only fourteen inches of water flowing over it. The captain saw no prospect of his steamer getting up-river that season.[2]

During the winter of 1889-90 extensive repairs were made to the **North West** at Cumberland. Eighty new frames were installed to replace those damaged during the navigation season of 1888; twenty to thirty new bottom planks were put in as well. Engineer James Levy gave her engines a complete overhauling before she sailed. In the 1890 season she was again under the command of Captain Smith.

The **North West** sailed from Cumberland House for Grand Rapids in June. Late in the month she took half a load up through the Roche Rouge and Demi-Charge rapids to the narrows of Cedar Lake, and then dropped down-river for the remainder of the cargo. She left Grand Rapids for the second time on June 30. Her cargo was mostly goods for the Hudson's Bay Company consigned for Battleford, Edmonton, and northern points. She reached Edmonton with 140 tons on July 2 after a voyage uneventful except for delays caused by wet weather and high winds.

When the steamer went down-river past Prince Albert, the newspaper reported that the **North West** would bring up the **Marquis,** beached at Cumberland since the 1887 season; then the lower river would be abandoned.

The new policy was dictated by the building of two branch railway lines from the main line of the Canadian Pacific Railway northward to the North Saskatchewan River; the terminals of the lines were to be Prince Albert and Edmonton respectively. The track-laying crews of the Qu'Appelle, Long Lake and Saskatchewan Railway and Steamboat Company reached Prince Albert on October 22, 1890. The Calgary and Edmonton railway was completed to Edmonton in the autumn of 1891. For the sternwheelers, with the impossibility of assuring consignees of delivery of goods, the competition of the railways spelled the end.

The two steamers came up to Prince Albert the first week in September, and were laid up for the winter. The newspaper reported that they would be overhauled, and predicted with unjustified optimism that they would have a busy season in 1891.

The **Marquis,** luxury steamer of the fleet, never sailed again. She remained on the riverbank and slowly disintegrated over many years.[3] For several years, her saloon was used as a dance hall. Finally, much of her lumber was used by a Mr. Billy McKay to build his house. As late as 1923, strips of her hull were photographed lying on the bank. Her boilers

The MARQUIS *hull, 1918.*

Saskatchewan Archives

The MARQUIS, *about 1900.*

were hauled away and used to hold power poles up-
right in a stretch of muskeg by a Canadian Utilities
Company engineer, Ed Kelly of Edmonton. The
Prince Albert city museum has a piece of the vessel's
flue, and her bell. The President of the Historical
Society of Prince Albert uses a gavel made of wood
from the **Marquis.**

209

Chapter 29

THE LAST YEARS OF
THE S.S. NORTH WEST

THE **NORTH WEST** spent her last years as a tramp steamer, picking up cargo where she could.

In 1891 the Prince Albert newspaper contained no reference to steamboats, so presumably the **North West** was not put in the water that season.

At the end of May, 1892, the **North West** made a trial run five miles upstream to the Sturgeon River; many Prince Albert citizens took the opportunity to enjoy a free boat trip. During June the paper publicized a coming excursion to Battleford for a round fare of five dollars, and on June 30 complained that only a dozen persons had taken advantage of the excursion. This would seem to have been the vessel's only earnings that season.

The following year, 1893, another excursion was organized, and "all the town and his wife" sailed aboard the **North West** for Battleford on Saturday, June 3, at 11:00 A.M. The boat docked off the ruins of Carlton House at 8:00 P.M., and settlers from as far as Duck Lake came aboard and danced until the anchor was weighed at 3:00 A.M. She arrived at Battleford on Monday afternoon, and while the excursionists spent a pleasant three days in the ex-capital of the Territories, the steamer went on to Pitt and back. She left Battleford on Friday morning, bucking a strong head wind which later blew her hard on a sand bar. Off Carlton, the excursionists presented Captain Dougal and Purser R. McGinn with illuminated addresses of thanks, lettered on birch bark. On Saturday evening the steamer arrived at the Prince Albert dock, "where our little company regretfully separated, and departed each unto his own habitation."

The same month the **North West** went back upstream to Battleford carrying flour for the Hudson's Bay Company. She then sailed down to Cumberland, and arrived back late in July, making slow time because the water was high and the current strong. She went on to Battleford and returned.

In 1894 the **North West** was again in service. She went up to Edmonton in June. According to the Edmonton **Bulletin,** at the sound of her whistle citizens were to be seen hurrying from their respective places of business to the riverbank at the rear of Jasper Avenue. The **North West** came in sight, flying her bunting. She carried some passengers, but machinery for the Moore and McDougall mill constituted most of her cargo.

While in Edmonton she was chartered for a short excursion, and 150 people took the boat trip. She also brought 200 tons of coal from the mine to Edmonton.

The **North West's** cargo for Battleford consisted of 37 barrels of lager beer, 5,500 feet of lumber, 24,000 shingles, 3,000 bushels of oats, and 10 tons of sundries. She had a tedious voyage down. On a gravel bed forty miles above Battleford, she had to unload most of her cargo to lighten her. After taking her remaining cargo to Battleford, she returned for what she had left.

En route to Cumberland House in mid-July, she had an accident in the rapids at Cole's Falls and had to return to Prince Albert for repairs. She arrived back in Prince Albert on August 20, and made at least one more trip to Battleford that season.

In 1895, the newspapers along the river made no reference to the **North West,** so she must not have been in operation.

In 1896, at the end of June, the Edmonton **Bulletin** described an excursion of 300 people to Fort Saskatchewan aboard the **North West.** The steamer then returned down-river. She arrived back in Edmonton from Prince Albert on August 2. Her cargo, at least as far as Pitt, had consisted of 45,000 feet of lumber and 1,000 sacks of flour. The boat, which had left Prince Albert on July 18, had been detained by contrary winds for five days. On August 1, at Sucker Creek Rapids, she had struck a rock which tore all the paddles off her wheel, but these had been repaired.

The last reference to the **North West** that season said that the Hudson's Bay Company Commissioner had made the boat available free of charge to the local Hospital Ladies' Aid. Then she was drawn up on the bank in the Ross Flats in Edmonton.

Ernest Brown collection—Alberta Archives

The NORTH WEST *at Edmonton, 1896.*

The S.S. **North West** sailed on her last voyage on August 17, 1899, during a flood. On August 14-15 the Saskatchewan River rose twenty-six feet, and flooded Ross Flats, where the sternwheeler had been beached three seasons before. On the afternoon of the 17th she broke from her moorings. Half the people of Edmonton town lined the high embankment above the river valley to see the old steamer go by. The piers of the Low Level Bridge were under construction, and were submerged by the flood waters. It looked at first as though the **North West** might pass between, but she struck a pier with a crushing sound, tearing out some of her innards. Now, only the upper deck and pilot house were above water. Two days later, she was seen passing Saddle Lake. Such was the end of the last of the sternwheel steamboats which plied the Saskatchewan from Grand Rapids to Edmonton.

The last meeting of the shareholders of the Winnipeg and Western Transportation Company was held in Winnipeg on March 4, 1901. At the meeting a motion was passed authorizing that the assets of the Company be transferred to the Hudson's Bay Company, the sole body to which the transportation company was indebted.[1]

Chapter 30

WHERE DID THE CAPTAINS GO?

THE SASKATCHEWAN riverboats were beached one by one in the years from 1886.

All the captains who had struggled against the perversity of the Saskatchewan River were Americans who, before coming to the Canadian Northwest, had had extensive experience on the rivers of the Mississippi system. Wherever they had originated along that river system, they had all gravitated toward the upper Mississippi, with Minneapolis-St. Paul as headquarters. Most had been on Red River boats carrying cargoes to Fort Garry (later Winnipeg) before moving on to the Saskatchewan River. This was one of the last of the larger rivers on the North American continent where sternwheelers were used. Everywhere, networks of railway lines had displaced the rivers as routes of transportation. When the steamboat era ended on the Saskatchewan, what became of the river captains?

Captain John Griggs, former captain of the **Northcote,** was dead. Captain Frank Aymond had retired to a farm four miles above Neche, on the Pembina River, in 1876.

215

The steamer NORTH WEST *as the photographer caught a view of her on the Saskatchewan River in 1896.*

Ernest Brown collection—Alberta Archives

Two of the captains returned to St. Paul. Captain James W. Lauderdale, on the Saskatchewan River part of the 1883 season, had been recalled to St. Paul by the death of two of his children from typhoid fever. He remained in that city, engaging first in business and later becoming a policeman. He died in 1904.

Captain Jerry Webber settled in the same city. As a boy, he had run away from home to become a cabin boy on an Ohio River boat, and he followed the river life all his days. The story has been already told of his superb piloting of the **Fanny Harris** to bring Sherman's Battery down the Minnesota River at the outbreak of the American Civil War. After he left the Saskatchewan, his last command was a small excursion steamer called the **Minnehaha,** which plied up-river from St. Paul a few miles to Minnehaha Falls. In the last summer of his life, at the age of eighty-six, he was still in command of the riverboat. He died on September 17, 1908.

Captain John B. Davis was commodore of the fleet of the Winnipeg and Western Transportation Company on the Saskatchewan for two seasons, 1883 and 1884. He returned to the Mississippi River, where his name had been a byword for his attempts to run boats on what was virtually dry land. His last command was aboard the **Sidney,** in 1887. When the owners decided to move this steamboat to the lower river and did not leave Captain Davis in command, he felt he had a grievance and retired from the river.

Captain Davis was succeeded on the Saskatchewan

by Captain James Sheets. As he was a very popular captain, it seems strange that his subsequent career is not known, and this suggests that he might possibly have died shortly after the 1888 season.

The last years of Aaron Raymond Russell are well documented, thanks to a life insurance policy he had taken out many years earlier. When it matured in 1915, the St. Paul office of the insurance company was searching for Russell without success. The St. Paul financier and railway builder, J. J. Hill, became interested in the search, having been a friend of Russell's half a century earlier. Hill placed advertisements in newspapers throughout the United States, and Captain Russell was found in an old folks' home in California.

The reader will recall that Russell was one of the river captains who had gone on the Nile expedition in the early winter of 1884. Back on the Saskatchewan, at the end of the 1885 season and with poor prospects for further employment as a riverman, he had changed his way of life. He had settled in California and become a fruit grower. Russell and his second wife were happy to receive the $300 insurance policy.

Captain Russell was a conscientious diarist, or so it would seem. The log of the United States army engineers' boat, the **C. F. Caffrey,** for the season he was in command, has been preserved. His diary of the Nile expedition appeared in 1916 among the articles by George B. Merrick published in the **Saturday Evening Post,** of Burlington, Iowa.

The last three of the captains, Dougal, Smith,

and Segers, after leaving the Saskatchewan, went on to skipper boats on the Athabasca-Mackenzie river systems for the Hudson's Bay Company. The first of these, Captain Julius Dougal, was captain of the **Marquis** for three years, 1885-1887, and of the **North West** in 1893 and perhaps for one or two other seasons. He would seem to have been captain of the **Wrigley** on the Mackenzie River.

Captain John H. Smith had a part in the building of the **Grahame** on the lower Athabaska and of the **Wrigley** on the Lake Athabasca-Mackenzie River system. This was in the middle years of the 1880's. He was back on the Saskatchewan again as captain of the **North West** for the season of 1889 and 1890. Later he farmed in Birds Hill Municipality in Manitoba. He died on May 29, 1917, in Winnipeg where he was attending a conference. The delegates were touring the city water works when he was struck down by a sudden heart attack. Captain Smith was in his 78th year.

The last of the captains, John Scribner Segers, indubitably sailed on more rivers than any other river captain in history. Before he came to the Saskatchewan, he had been on the upper Mississippi, the Minnesota, and the Red River. In 1885 he moved to Athabasca Landing under a contract with the Hudson's Bay Company to build and operate a stern-wheeler for three years on the upper Athabasca. The vessel he built was called the **Athabasca.** He remained in charge for a dozen years. For at least one season he was on the **Grahame,** which plied the lower river, and he also had experience on the **Wrigley.**

219

Gold was discovered in the Klondike, and in the summer of 1897, Captain Segers led a party of fourteen men in boats down the Athabasca and Mackenzie rivers to the Arctic Red River. The party then split into two groups. The Segers group went over the watershed the following spring and down the Porcupine River, which enters the Yukon River at Fort Yukon, and from there they took a river steamer to travel up to Dawson City. The party had been traveling a year to reach the gold fields.

In the Klondike, Captain Segers soon returned to the river life as captain of the **Sovereign.** In 1903 he invested his savings in a sternwheeler, which he named the **Quickstep.** On one of his trips down the Yukon River he had his boat anchored in the harbor at Nome, Alaska. A tidal wave, caused by a subterranean earthquake, hit the harbor, depositing the **Quickstep** on top of a dockside warehouse. Not only had he lost his life's savings, but he had a lawsuit on his hands for $1,500, property damage to the warehouse.

Captain Segers had one more adventure after leaving the Yukon River. A year or two later, in early spring, he was traveling with two companions in the mountains of Idaho. A snowslide came down the mountain and entombed them. Captain Segers was rescued many hours later, but the two other men were never seen again.

The captain died in the spring of 1909 at Rossland, British Columbia.

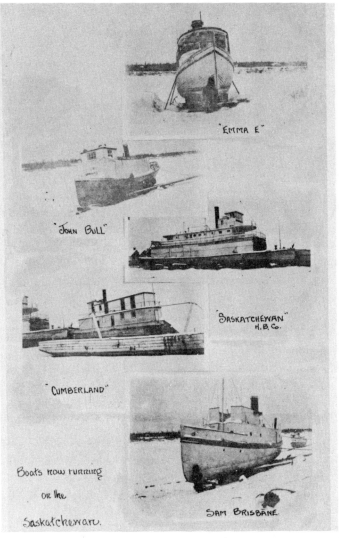

"EMMA E"

"JOHN BULL"

"SASKATCHEWAN" H.B. Co.

"CUMBERLAND"

Boats now running on the Saskatchewan.

SAM BRISBANE.

Public Archives of Canada

Boats running on the Saskatchewan in 1908.

221

Chapter 31

THE LAST RIVERBOATS

OVER THE YEARS, other steamboats have plied the Saskatchewan River, sternwheelers and screw steamers, but none has been of the length and tonnage of the early steamers; nor has any of them regularly plied the length of the river. Some have been local excursion boats, or tugs for moving barges.

The name of Captain H. H. Ross appears frequently in later navigation history. He operated boats first out of Medicine Hat, and later out of The Pas. His first boat was the **Assiniboia,** which sailed from Medicine Hat in 1905 and was destroyed by ice the following spring at Cedar Lake. In 1908 he again sailed from his home port on a 130-foot sternwheeler, the **City of Medicine Hat.** She came to grief at Saskatoon when she struck the pier of a bridge. She had gone out of control after hitting a telephone wire strung across the river and snagging a piece of it on her rudder.

The Dominion Government appointed Captain Ross fisheries inspector, with headquarters at The Pas. He had the **Sam Brisbin,** a screw steamer, built

Saskatoon Star-Phoenix

The ill-fated CITY OF MEDICINE HAT.

Western Development Museum

Wreck of the CITY OF MEDICINE HAT, *Saskatoon, June 7, 1908.*

at Collingwood, Ontario. In 1911 Captain Ross had a second boat built, **The Pas**. He organized the Ross Navigation Company, which in time operated six vessels. Best known, in addition to the **Brisbin**, were the **Notin**, the **Tobin**, and the **Nipawin**. These boats operated from Cumberland Lake to Cedar Lake, and up navigable tributaries such as the Carrot River.

At Prince Albert the second boat bearing the name **Alberta** was built. She was the only boat ever to go down Grand Rapids. Other boats operating out of Prince Albert in the first two decades of the twentieth century were the **George V** and the **Saskatchewan**. The latter vessel was owned by the Hudson's Bay Company and was used to transport supplies from Prince Albert to Cumberland and The Pas.

At The Pas, the Finger Lumber Company, and its successor, the Pas Lumber Company, operated river steamers from 1912 until 1953. The first of these was a sidewheeler, the **C. R. Smith**. Other vessels built by the lumber company were the **Jack Winton**, and later, the 120-foot **David N. Winton**. This boat's machinery came from the **George V** which was destroyed in 1919 when she failed to rise during the spring break-up.

With the big copper strike at Mandy, Manitoba, in 1917, there was a need to move the ore to the railhead at The Pas. For the next eight seasons ore was carried by water from Sturgeon Landing, across Cumberland Lake, out the Bigstone River, and down the Saskatchewan to The Pas. The **Nipawin**, a sternwheeler of 86.8 feet in length, was built for the Ross Navigation Company to move the ore barges

Ted Tadda photo

The last sternwheel steamer at The Pas, 1953.

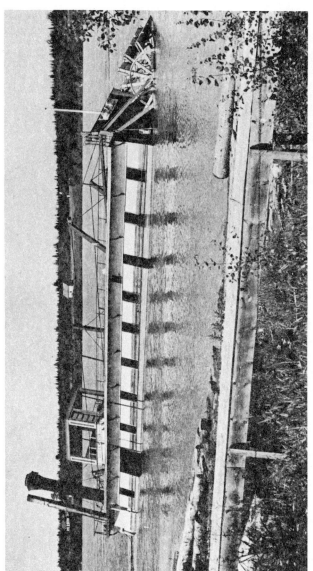

Richard Harrington photo

Wreck of the DAVID N. WINTON, *1954.*

over the water route. Her career as an ore vessel ended in 1925 when the railway was extended from The Pas to Flin Flon. During those years she had transported over 26,000 tons of copper ore.

The **David N. Winton** for over thirty years pulled log rafts down the Carrot River. When she was sunk by the action of ice in the spring of 1954, the last of the sternwheel steamers had disappeared from the river.

NOTES

1. THE RIVER

[1]C. J. Brydges to F. H. Ennis, September 19, 1879. In *Reports, correspondence and surveys . . . improvement of the Saskatchewan River for the purpose of navigation.* Canadian Sessional Paper, No. 138, 1885. Hereafter cited C.S.P., No. 138, 1885.

2. EARLY SURVEYS OF THE RIVER

[1]Palliser, John. *Exploration-British North America. Further papers.* (London, 1860) pp. 36-37.

[2]Willson, Beckles. *Life of Lord Strathcona and Mount Royal.* (London, 1915) pp. 347-348.

[3]Dictionary of national biography. Also Spry, Irene M. *The Palliser expedition, an account of John Palliser's British North American Expedition, 1857-1860.* (Toronto, Macmillan, 1963) See index for references to Blakiston.

[4]Hind, H. Y. *Narrative of the Canadian Red River exploring expedition of 1857, and of the Assiniboine and Saskatchewan exploring expedition of 1858.* (London, 1860) pp. 472-73.

[5]*The Nor'Wester,* Dec. 11, 1865. Also quoted in Russell, A. J. *The Red River country, Hudson's Bay and North West Territories.* (Montreal, 1870.) 3d ed. p. 63. The journal of a missionary from The Pas, J. J. Smith, who accompanied Munn and Hutchinson from that point as far as Fort à la Corne is to be found in the microfilmed records of the Church Missionary Society, Records and correspondence, Reel 22.

[6]E. A. Burbank to C. J. Brydges, December 19, 1883, and November 28, 1884. In C.S.P. No. 138, 1885.

[7]Klotz, Otto. *Report on exploratory survey to Hudson's Bay,* 1884. In *Annual Report* of the Department of the Interior, Part II, C.S.P., No. 13, 1885, pp. 13-35. His diary of the survey, a detailed map, and also a newspaper series by his surveyor, John A. Cadenhead, are in the Public Archives of Canada. I have been unable to locate his photographs, although some have appeared in publications.

[8]Voligny, L. R. *Report on the survey of the North Saskatchewan River from Edmonton to Lake Winnipeg, 1910-1915.* (Ottawa, 1916?) A microfilm copy was examined in the Saskatchewan Archives.

3. COMPANY CHANGES ITS TRANSPORT ORGANIZATION

[1]Macoun, John. *Manitoba and the great North West.* (Guelph, 1882) pp. 580-82. According to the *Moorhead Advocate* (as quoted in the *Manitoba Daily Free Press,* April 7, 1877) the quantity of cargo carried by steamboats on the Red River in three successive seasons was as follows: 1873 — 23,613,036 lbs.; 1874 — 37,626,200 lbs.; 1875 — 76, 078, 680 lbs.

[2]House of Commons. *Debates.* 1878 (March 11) p. 955.

³Smith, Henry B. "Memorandum on the portages and streams between Lakes Winnipeg, Manitoba, Winnipegosis, and the River Saskatchewan at Cedar Lake. From *Report on surveys made . . . in 1873*. In Sandford Fleming's *Report of progress on the explorations and surveys up to January, 1874*. (Ottawa, 1874) pp. 259-62.

⁴*Manitoban*, May 18, 1872.

⁵Munro, W. F. "Winnipegosis". In *Rose - Belford's Canadian Monthly and National Review*, v. 3, July-December, 1879, p. 479. Munro says incorrectly that the woodpiles were intended for the S.S. *Colvile*.

⁶*Manitoba Daily Free Press*, March 30, 1876.

4. FIRST STEAMBOAT

¹McFarlane, Roderick. Correspondence. In the Public Archives of Canada, Ottawa. The letter quoted was addressed to Roderick McFarlane. Letters from this collection hereafter cited McFarlane Correspondence.

²See Merrick, Geo. B. "Steamboats and steamboatmen of the upper Mississippi"; a series of articles in the *Saturday Evening Post* (Burlington, Iowa); issue of May 13, 1916. (Microfilm).

³*Bulletin*, January 8, 1883.

⁴Robt. Hamilton in a letter to Chief Commissioner Donald A. Smith, August 5, 1873, described the wreck. H.B.C. Arch. A. 12/14.

⁵*Manitoban*, August 30, 1873.

⁶Church Missionary Society. Records and correspondence.

⁷Canada. Geological Survey. *Reports of progress for 1873-74*. p. 44.

⁸Alfred R. C. Selwyn to Sandford Fleming, January 9, 1874. In Fleming, *Op. cit.* p. 258.

5. S.S. *Northcote*

¹For a description of the building of the *Northcote* see the following correspondence in H.B.C. Arch.: Donald A. Smith to Wm. Armit, November 24, 1873; John H. McTavish to Donald A. Smith, November 5, 1873; Captain F. Aymond to J. H. McTavish, November 5, 1873, A. 12/14; also Donald A. Smith to Wm. Armit, April 20, 1874, A. 12/15; also James A. Grahame to Wm. Armit, June 15, 1874, D. 13/1, fo. 7; also James A. Grahame to Wm. Armit, July 29, 1874, D. 13/1, fos. 13-14; also James A. Grahame to Wm. Armit, Aug. 24, 1874, D. 13/1, fo. 44d; also Robert Hamilton to James A. Grahame, August 15, 1874, D. 14/12, fos. 140-142.

²Shipping Register of the Port of Winnipeg. Microfilm copies may be found in the Public Archives of Canada and in the Manitoba Archives. Hereafter cited as Shipping Register.

³Church Missionary Society. Records and correspondence.

⁴*Ibid*.

⁵H.B.C. *Report to shareholders, November 24, 1874*.

⁶Steele, S. B. *Forty years in Canada*. (Toronto, 1918) p. 70.

⁷Alex Matheson to McFarlane. McFarlane Correspondence.

⁸As quoted in the *Manitoban*, October 3, 1874.

6. NAVIGATION SEASONS 1875 AND 1876.

¹Robert Hamilton to McFarlane, August 11, 1875. In McFarlane Correspondence. See also *The Standard* (Winnipeg), August 28, 1875.

[2]Robert Hamilton to McFarlane, *Op. cit.* and below.
[3]Robert Hamilton to McFarlane, December 23, 1875. In Mc-
Farlane Correspondence.
[4]James A. Grahame to William Armit, August 11, 1876, H.B.C.
Arch. D. 14/15. The *Northcote* may have waited for a rise in the
water and got up to Carlton, but there is no evidence that she
succeeded in reaching her destination.
[5]The account of the *Northcote's* voyages in 1876 is largely based
on information supplied by the Hudson's Bay Company's archives.
See also the Company's *Reports to shareholders of November 29,
1876* and *June 25, 1878.* In Winnipeg the *Daily Free Press* twice
reported (on August 9 and September 1) that the *Northcote* was
aground in a rapid, and these reports were promptly denied by
Company officials. The paper said that 5,000 packages for the
Saskatchewan River were lying at Grand Rapids.
[6]James A. Grahame to William Armit, December 5, 1876. H.B.C.
Arch. D. 13/2, fo. 194.
[7]O-ge-mas-es. "Steamboating for the H.B.C. on the Saskatchewan."
The Beaver, April, 1922, p. 21. The writer gives the year of the
incident as 1877, but I believe it could only relate to 1876 and to
Captain Aymond.

7. Navigation Season 1877

[1]The Company was incorporated at $200,000. The incorporators
were the following: James Sutherland, William Forbes Alloway,
and Thomas B. Miller, all of Winnipeg; John Wright Sifton, Selkirk; and Peter Johnson Brown, Ingersoll, Ont.
[2]Canada. Department of Marine. *Annual report for 1877.* C.S.P.,
No. 1, 1878. Information on the tonnage of vessels inspected,
wrecks, etc. may be found in the annual reports of subsequent
years. For Abell's appointment, birthdate, etc. see *Annual report
for 1892,* Board of steamboat inspection, inspectors of boilers and
machinery.
[3]*Return of all papers concerning the granting of a charter to the
Hudson's Bay Company, to construct a tramway around the north
shore of Grand Rapids.* C.S.P., No. 139, 1882. For a description of
the tramway remains consult Ron Vastokas "The Grand Rapid
Portage." *The Beaver*, Autumn, 1961, outfit 292, pp. 22-26.
[4]Munro, *Op. cit.*
[5]Morgan, H. J. *Canadian men and women of the time.* (Toronto,
1898) pp. 640-641.
[6]Dufferin and Ava, Marchioness of. *My Canadian journal.* (London, 1891) p. 355.
[7]Moberly, Walter. *The rocks and rivers of British Columbia* (Vancouver, 1885) p. 99. Although officially opened in September, the
tramway was not completed until the second week of October.
[8]"The iron steamer constructed in England for the Hudson's Bay
Company is expected daily." *Manitoba Daily Free Press,* August
18, 1876.
[9]*Manitoba Daily Free Press,* October 17, 1877.
[10]Shipping Register.
[11]MacKay, Elsie. *Selkirk's 75th anniversary.* (Selkirk, 1957) p. 87

[12]James A. Grahame to Wm. L. Hardisty, 21 December, 1877. H.B.C. Arch. D. 13/11, fos. 10d-11.
[13]H.B.C. *Report to shareholders, November 27th, 1877.*
[14]McTavish, G. S. "Report on the working of the steamer Northcote season 1877." 16 November, 1877. H.B.C. Arch. A. 12/16.
[15]"Report of the Working of the Steamer Northcote, Season 1877." G. S. McTavish, November 1, 1877; London Inward Correspondence. Hudson's Bay Company records, as quoted in Stanley, G. F. G. *The birth of Western Canada* (Toronto, 1960) p. 185.

8. NAVIGATION SEASON 1878

[1]Alexander Matheson to James A. Grahame, 17 October, 1878. H.B.C. Arch. D. 14/21.
[2]Canada. Department of Marine. *Annual report for 1878.*
[3]H.B.C. *Report to shareholders, November 26, 1878.*
[4]Matheson. *Op. cit.* Letters to Grahame dated July 26, July 27, August 30, and October 17, 1878.
[5]Words indecipherable in original letter.
[6]The letter was dated August 9, 1878. In McFarlane Correspondence.

9. NAVIGATION SEASON 1879

[1]The steamer's difficulties climbing Thorburn Rapids would seem to have been the genesis of a rumor in Winnipeg that she was on the rocks near Fort à la Corne. *Manitoba Daily Free Press,* August 20 and 22, 1879.
[2]The lake and river steamers earned $118.00 for transporting 18 farm instructors and their baggage from Winnipeg to the Lower Fort, and $8,587.75 from that port to the south branch. The Hudson's Bay Company also was paid $3,624.72 for freighting the cargo by cart from the Muskoday Reserve. See Canada. Department of Indian Affairs. *Annual report for 1880.* C.S.P., No. 14, 1881, pp. 285 and 289.
[3]*Winnipeg Daily Times,* September 22, 1879, quoting the *Selkirk Inter-Ocean* of September 19. See also Alexander Matheson to James A. Grahame, 13 September, 1879.
[4]The information on the *Lily* is taken from the issues of the *Saskatchewan Herald* for 1879 unless otherwise specified.
[5]Manitoba History Scrapbook, v. 1, 1884-1904, p. 252. In Manitoba Archives.
[6]H.B.C. *Report to shareholders, July 6, 1880.*
[7]*Bulletin,* November 5, 1881.
[8]As quoted in the *Winnipeg Daily Times,* September 5, 1879.
[9]C. J. Brydges to the Hon. H. L. Langevin, September 28, 1880. C.S.P., No. 138, 1885, p. 9.
[10]Munro. *Op. cit.* pp. 479-80.

10. NAVIGATION SEASON 1880

[1]Sutherland, Alexander. *A summer in prairie land.* (Toronto, 1881) p. 138.
[2]H.B.C. *A general court of the Governor and Company of Adventurers (etc), held, 6th July, 1880.*
[3]*Winnipeg Daily Times,* June 12, 1880.

[4]*Saskatchewan Herald*, June 21, 1880.
[5]Laurence Clarke to James A. Grahame, August 2, 1880. H.B.C. Arch. D. 14/23.
[6]*Saskatchewan Herald*, November 29, 1880.
[7]Greene, David L. *An historical sketch, Christ Church, The Pas.* (The Pas, 1931)
[8]H.B.C. *Report to shareholders, November 23, 1880.*
[9]C. J. Brydges to the Hon. H. L. Langevin, September 28, 1880. In C.S.P., No. 138, 1885.
[10]C. J. Brydges to the Right Hon. Sir John A. Macdonald, October 11, 1880. In C.S.P., No. 138, 1885.

11. NAVIGATION SEASON 1881

[1]Merrick. *Op. cit.*, issues of July 4, 1914, and May 25, 1918; also *Ottawa Free Press*, October 15, 1884, "Off to Egypt."
[2]*Saskatchewan Herald*, October 17, 1881. For an account of the Governor General's tour see Williams, W.H. *Manitoba and the North West.* (Toronto, 1882) Williams accompanied the vice-regal party.
[3]*Winnipeg Daily Times*, September 12, 1881.
[4]*Saskatchewan Herald*, October 3, 1881.

12. WINNIPEG STEAMBOAT COMPANY ON THE SASKATCHEWAN

[1]See Chapter 7.
[2]The incorporators were: John Turnbull, Montreal merchant; Charles W. Black, Montreal accountant; A. G. B. Bannatyne, Winnipeg merchant; Hon. James McKay, St. James contractor; J. H. Ashdown, Winnipeg merchant; W. H. Lyon, Winnipeg merchant; E. V. Holcombe, St. Paul, Minnesota steamboat man; Sedley Blanchard, Winnipeg barrister. Lyon, Blanchard, Holcombe, Turnbull, and Black were listed as the Provisional Directors.
[3]For an account of ownership of Red River steamboats in 1878, see Macoun, *Op. cit.* pp. 582-83.
[4]The incorporators were the following: Andrew Allan and A. T. Drummond of Montreal together with Peter McArthur, William Robinson, Duncan McArthur, C. J. Brydges, James Graham, C. S. Drummond and Alex McArthur of Winnipeg and William Lawson, Andrew Wilson and William McKenzie of Dundee, Scotland.
[5]The persons incorporating the new company were the following: Hugh McK. Sutherland, H. N. Ruttan, Amos Rowe, and P. J. Brown all of Winnipeg, and Duncan MacMillan, M.P., of London, Ontario. See Morgan's *Dominion annual register for 1882*, pp. 271-72.
[6]C. J. Brydges to F. H. Ennis, August 15, 1882. C.S.P., No. 138, 1885.

13. TRANSFER OF VESSELS TO THE SASKATCHEWAN

[1]*Winnipeg Daily Times*, April 30, 1881.
[2]H.B.C. Arch. C. 7/91.
[3]For accounts of the wreck see the *Winnipeg Daily Times*, September 28 and October 11, 1881; also the *Manitoba Free Press*, September 21, 1881.

[4]*Bulletin*, July 29, 1882.
[5]*Winnipeg Daily Times*, May 16, May 19, and July 9, 1881.
[6]Shipping Register.
[7]Merrick. *Op. cit.* issues of April 22 and June 4, 1916; *Ottawa Free Press*, October 15, 1884, "Off to Egypt."
[8]Herriott, Marion H. "Steamboat transportation on the Red River." *Minnesota History*, v. 21, 1940, p. 263.

14. NAVIGATION SEASON 1882

[1]The figure for tonnage is of freight brought into the Saskatchewan country through Grand Rapids. It does not include local freight moved between river ports, or any of the export freight. The export would only be furs and though a valuable cargo, would not contribute much to the total tonnage of freight.
[2]*Saskatchewan Herald*, August 5, 1882.
[3]Church Missionary Society. Records and Correspondence.

15. THE CUT-OFF

[1]Klotz. *Op. cit.*
[2]*Ibid.*
[3]Laurence Clarke to James A. Grahame, May 21, 1882. H.B.C. Arch. D.14/28.
[4]C.S.P., No. 138, 1885, p. 21.
[5]Veteran pilot, Joseph Favell, came up-river by rowboat late in October, and was quoted as being of the opinion that the boats could have got through by the Sturgeon River route as he had found three feet of water in the shallowest places. *Saskatchewan Herald*, November 11, 1882.
[6]In Winnipeg, after the return of the steamboat crews, Captain Sheets was quoted as saying there were only 500 tons at Cumberland. *Winnipeg Daily Times*, October 26, 1882.
[7]See King's reports in *Annual reports* of the Department of the Interior, C.S.P., No. 23, 1883, p. 15; C.S.P., No. 13, 1885, p. 9.

16. RIVER IMPROVEMENTS

[1]This chapter is based mostly on the correspondence between C. J. Brydges and officials of the Dominion Department of Public Works, to be found in C.S.P., No. 158, 1885.
[2]On the point of a sharp bend in the river, as late as 1912, a capstan was to be seen. The point was known as Capstan Point.
[3]In the House of Commons in the sessions of 1881 and 1882 during the debate on the supply vote questions were asked of Sir Hector Langevin relative to improvements on the Saskatchewan River. He suggested that the total cost of improvements would be about $32,000; the government would spend about $10,000 each on wing dams at Thorburn Rapids and Cole's Falls while the Hudson's Bay Company would invest $6,000 on each of the two piers. See House of Commons. *Debates.*
[4]*Saskatchewan Herald*, September 6, 1886.
[5]House of Commons. *Debates*, 1888. p. 1655-56; also in Estimates of the Department of Public Works (Harbours & Rivers) for the financial year ending 30 June, 1888, p. 159. Examined in the Public Archives of Canada.

On Cole's Falls more human effort and tax-payers' money have been expended with less to show than on any other point on the river. Here, in 1913, the City of Prince Albert began construction of a large dam to supply electrical power. Not sufficient study had been made of the site prior to construction, and it was found that water seeped through the soil under the dam. When the structure was about half completed, work was abandoned, and it may be seen to this day in its unfinished state. The city continued to pay debentures on the unfortunate undertaking for nearly fifty years after its abandonment.

[6]For annual expenditures see the *Annual reports* of the Department of Public Works.

[7]*Bulletin,* August 3, 1896.

17. NAVIGATION SEASON 1883

[1]C.S.P., No. 138, 1885, pp. 26-27.

[2]*Saskatchewan Herald,* July 7, 1883.

[3]Merrick, Geo. B. *Old times on the Upper Mississippi.* (Cleveland, 1909) pp. 269, 283, 292.

[4]Merrick Geo. B. "Steamboats and steamboating on the upper Mississippi." Issue of May 8, 1915.

[5]Lass, W. E. *History of steamboating on the upper Missouri River.* (Lincoln, 1962) pp. 125-26.

[6]The *Princess* did not arrive from Winnipeg until June 21. The ice in the northern part of Lake Winnipeg was later than usual in leaving the lake.

[7]Lorne, Marquis of. *Canadian Pictures.* (London 1885) pp. 175-76.

[8]Minnesota Historical Society. Scrap Books, v. 35, pp. 109-10.

[9]Captain John B. Davis to James A. Grahame, October 18, 1883. H.B.C. Arch. F. 37/3. See also a long interview with Captain Davis reported in *Winnipeg Daily News,* October 12, 1883.

18. LAST VOYAGE OF THE *Lily*

[1]*Manitoba Free Press,* April 27, 1909; also letter and interview with his daughter, Mrs. J. H. Watson of Vancouver.

[2]*The Colonizer,* December, 1883. This four-page paper was issued by the Temperance Colonization Society.

[3]James A. Grahame to Thomas R. Smith, September 11, 1883. H.B.C. Arch. A.11/107.

[4]H.B.C. *General court of the Governor and' Company held, Tuesday, July 1, 1884.*

[5]C.S.P., No. 138, 1885, p. 31.

[6]The *Lily's* anchor rests in the Prince Albert Museum, donated by Mrs. E. L. Davis.

[7]*Saskatoon Star-Phoenix.* (I do not have the date of the interview other than it was in the summer of 1935.)

19. NAVIGATION SEASON 1884

[1]Board of Directors' meeting, March 8, 1884. H.B.C. Arch. F.36/1, pp. 93-94.

[2]James A. Grahame to Wm. Armit, July 15, 1884. H.B.C. Arch. D. 13/6, fos. 329-30, and fo. 342.

[3]According to Archie Ballantine's reminiscences the voyage took 17 days. Ballantine was foreman. See MacKay, *Op. cit.* p. 77.

[4]Board of Directors' meeting, November 26, 1884. H.B.C. Arch. F.36/1, pp. 104-105.
[5]Letter, November 29, 1884. H.B.C. Arch. B. 332/C/1.

20. SASKATCHEWAN CAPTAINS ON THE NILE

[1]This account is based on Captain Russell's diary published in four installments in the *Saturday Evening Post* of Burlington, Iowa, June 3-July 4, 1916, as part of the series on steamboating by Geo. B. Merrick. See the Ottawa papers for October 15, 1884, and March 21, 1885. Also Stacey, C.P., ed. *Records of the Nile voyageurs, 1884-1885.* (Toronto, 1959).

21. THE COAL FLEET

[1]Skelton, O. D. *Life and times of Sir Alexander Tilloch Galt.* (Toronto, 1920) p. 551.
[2]For fuller information about the coal fleet consult Johnston, Alexander. *Boats and barges on the Belly.* (Lethbridge, 1966).
[3]Higinbotham, J. D. *When the West was young.* (Toronto, 1933) pp. 108-09.
[4]Shipping Register. Also the source of the dimensions of the other vessels.
[5]*Dictionary of national biography;* also Patterson, Clara Burdett. *Angela Burdett-Coutts and the Victorians.* (London, 1953)
[6]Higinbotham clippings. In Glenbow Foundation.
[7]During this period the river below the confluence of the Oldman and Belly was called the Belly River. It was changed to the Oldman when that river proved to be the main stream.
[8]Skelton. *Op. cit.* p. 556.
[9]*Ibid.*

22. NAVIGATION SEASON 1885

[1]North West Mounted Police. Commissioner. *Report,* 1885.
[2]*Winnipeg Daily News,* April 4, 1885.
[3]*Ibid.* April 10, 1885.
[4]Canada. Department of Militia and Defence. *Report of Major-General Laurie, commanding base and lines of communication, upon matters in connection with the suppression of the rebellion.* (Ottawa 1887) Hereafter cited Maj.-Gen. Laurie's report.
[5]Canada. Department of Militia and Defence. *Report upon the suppression of the rebellion in the North West Territories.* (Ottawa, 1886) Appendix E: Lieut.-Col. Otter's report. p. 45, Hereafter cited Report upon suppression of rebellion.
[6]Captain Sheets turned the actual operational command of the *Northcote* over to Captain Segers. Sheets had attempted to leave overland with Otter's column as he wished to get to Prince Albert to get the navigation company's other boats into service. He was concerned about the freight for the season. The commandant of bases refused to allow Sheets to leave with Otter, and so he sailed with the *Northcote.*
[7]Maj.-Gen. Laurie's report.
[8]Report upon suppression of rebellion. See report of Deputy Surgeon-General T. G. Roddick, pp. 105-106.
[9]Maj.-Gen. Laurie's report.

23. THE BATTLE OF BATOCHE

[1]Correspondent to the *St. Paul Pioneer Press*. See his dispatch as printed in the *Winnipeg Daily News*, May 16, 1885. See also the account telegraphed to the Toronto *Globe* and later reprinted in *Canadian Pictorial & Illustrated War News* (Souvenir number).
[2]Report upon suppression of rebellion. See Captain Smith's report. pp. 39-42.
[3]*Ibid.* General Middleton's diary of events. p. 5.
[4]*General Middleton's defence: as contained in his parting address to the people of Canada.* (n.p., 1890) p. 4.
[5]The persons in the pilot house during the battle were Captain Segers, Captain Sheets and Purser Talbot. Segers was in charge and Sheets acted as pilot. Talbot handled a rifle and received slight flesh wounds in shoulder and ankle. Segers received a bullet in his coat sleeve. Dozens of bullets came through the thin walls and the windows of the house. According to Segers' obituary notice many years later, no less than ninety bullets were found embedded in a bale of hay bulwarking the pilot house. The rebels made the house a special target, for they were well aware that it was the vessel's most vulnerable point.

Archie Ballantine's version of the battle, based on hearsay and written many years later, was that Captain Sheets steered the boat lying on the floor looking through a hole cut for the purpose, and protected on either side by box stoves. Hitting the ferry cable, the *Northcote* was swung sideways and might have gone in towards the shore. The pilot house rang the engineer to reverse to get the boat back into midstream, but the man had fled to the hold. Dan Herce, the fireman, came to the rescue and backed the vessel into midstream again. (MacKay, *Op. Cit.,* p. 77).
[6]See Dumont's account as contained in Ouimet, Adolphe. *La verité sur la question métisse.* (Montréal, 1889) pp. 136-37.
[7]See the picture of the *Northcote* taken after Batoche.

24. TROOP TRANSPORTS

[1]Ballantine, Archie. "The story of Archie Ballantine, as told in his own words." *Northern Lights,* March, 1955, pp. 23-25.
[2]Hines, John. *Red Indians of the plains.* (London, 1915) pp. 206-07.
[3]Ballantine. *Op. cit.*
[4]*Bulletin,* August 1, 1885.

26. NAVIGATION SEASON 1886

[1]H. B. C. Arch. C. 7/91.
[2]McArthur, Peter. Recollections. In Manitoba Archives clipping file.
[3]*Saskatchewan Herald,* September 9, 1886.
[4]Winnipeg and Western Transportation Company. *Report to the Board of Directors,* April 11, 1887. H.B.C. Arch.

27. NAVIGATION SEASON 1887

[1]McArthur. *Op. cit.*
[2]H.B.C. Arch. D. 18/12, fos. 434a.-434d. Letter dated March 26, 1888.

28. Navigation Seasons 1888, 1889, and 1890

[1]H.B.C. Arch. F. 36/1, pp. 175-176.
[2]*Prince Albert Times,* August 16, 1889.
[3]On August 28, 1899, the same flood that carried away the *North West* at Edmonton would have carried away the *Marquis* at Prince Albert had the crest been two feet higher.

29. Last Years of the S.S. *North West*

[1]H.B.C. Arch. F. 36/1, pp. 243-44.

INDEX

CUMBERLAND HOUSE

THE

Kadoie Ch.

Big Stone R.

Cumberland Lake

Steamboat Ch. (formerly the Sturgeon R.)

Angling Ch.

Big Moqar Bar

The CUT-OFF

Sipanok Channel

Squaw Rapids

Thorburn (Tobin's) Rapids

Pemmican Point

Big Birch Is.

Pasquia Hills

Jump-off Rapid

Victoria R.

Crooked Rapid

Eya Rapid

Dog Rump Rapid

Moose Rapids

Stony Bar Rapid

FORT EDMONTON

FORT PITT

NORTH SAS-

KATCHEWAN

BATTLEFORD

CARLTON HOUSE

PRI ALBER

BAT

Fish C

Clarke's Cr

SASKATOON

Battle River

SOUTH SASKATCHEWAN RIVER

Red Deer River

Bow River

Oldman R.

LETHBRIDGE

MEDICINE HAT

Saskatchewan Landing

STEAMBOATS on